D0903626

TECHNICAL ANALYSIS
IN COMMODITIES

TECHNICAL ANALYSIS IN COMMODITIES

P. J. KAUFMAN

A RONALD PRESS
PUBLICATION

JOHN WILEY & SONS
New York   Chichester
Brisbane   Toronto

This book is dedicated to my father,
for his guidance.

Library of Congress Cataloging in Publication Data:

Main entry under title:
Technical analysis in commodities.

"A Ronald Press publication."
Includes index.
1. Commodity exchanges—Addresses, essays,
lectures. I. Kaufman, Perry J.

HG6046.T4   332.6'44   79-19513
ISBN 0-471-05627-8

Printed in the United States of America

10 9 8 7 6 5 4 3 2 1

FOREWORD

Commodity futures trading philosophically may well require the three human disciplines in Huxley's definition of "charity" in his *Perennial Philosophy*: humility, tranquility, and detachment. Hartley touches on detachment in the lead article of this book when he says, "Get yourself far enough above the movements and directions of prices so you can develop sound strategy." Lofton's article implies that technical analysis can be the instrument to lessen "uncomfortable decision-making situations," that is, it can give the mind tranquility enough to relax, resolve, and then act. And if humility has to do with removing macho so that the trader may see through his personal fog to the truth of the next trend probability—Kaufman and a half-dozen of his fellow writers herein make diverse contributions toward this end "by application of specific, well-defined rules or equations."

But why the publication of this and scores of other works on commodity futures trading over the past few years? Why the wide readership and interest in what is often called an arcane subject? The answers are simple and fundamental.

First, neither commodities in general nor cash and futures commodity trading in particular are mysterious. Both have been a basic part of human life since the dawn of written history. One of the first and most famous grain trades was young Joseph's deal with the Pharaoh which saved Egypt's breadbasket in ancient biblical days.

As for futures, oriental businessmen became interested in this improvement over cash trading almost three centuries ago. Japanese records indicate that sub-rosa rice futures were traded as early as 1697 and legalized in 1730. England experimented with futures in the 1820s. Futures trading in the United States came into being in 1865 on the Chicago Board of Trade and was well established in other cities by 1920.

And today, an ever-increasing number of a better-educated populace is becoming aware that futures trading in the form of hedging and speculation is a part of the economic facts of modern life.

Admittedly, commercial banking, investment banking, and securities trading were essential to the development of the capital needs of the industrial revolution. However, commodities have always been the backbone of this commerce and the fundamental building blocks of all trade. In short, most of what we see, eat, drive, wear, and live in are commodities, or packages of commodities, like our houses and automobiles.

It's true that the big explosion in futures activity is a product of the second half of the twentieth century. Since 1960, futures volume has multiplied by some 1500%, from 7.8 million trades annually to 117 million in 1978, and it is still growing. Another more unpopular way of expressing the explosion is in terms of the extended value of these contracts. In dollars the expansion was from a total worth of 42 billion in 1960 to over 2 trillion by 1978, an increase of 5000%.

So it's small wonder that both business people and public traders are hungry for such books as you now hold in hand. Both education and published experimentation in commodities have been neglected. Two contributors to this volume, Testa and Hargrove, touch on this point by saying, "The formal analysis of commodity price movement is still in its infancy when compared to the applications of Markov chains, Fourier, and special analyses which have been made in the securities markets." Thus the special value of this book, of such educational efforts as the lecture and correspondence courses of the Futures Industry Association, and of the recently established department for the study of futures trading by Columbia University—with the help of the Commodity Futures Exchange (COMEX) of New York.

Most of us are told that if we lack satisfactory worldly success, we shall assuredly receive our reward in heaven. But it's more fun to gather some rosebuds along the way. One of the small pleasures of this writer is that his dream of a truly viable futures market, conceived while an account executive with Merrill Lynch in the 1950s, has come to pass. Through all those days of wars and rumors of wars, depression, recession, and now inflation, the commodity futures markets have confounded their critics—private, public, and governmental. The impossible only took a little longer when the Chicago Mercantile Exchange under the leadership of retired president Everette B. Harris brought on live animal trading, and later foreign currency futures during the chairmanship of Leo Melamed. The Chicago Board of Trade succeeded with the first interest-rate contract, designed by Richard Sandor. Financial instruments have become the fastest growing segment of the futures markets.

In each of these cases the very real services of risk transference for business hedgers, fair-price discovery for the public, and profit opportunity for the investor/speculator furnished the economic justification for success.

As to the future of commodity futures trading, the final breakthrough has come. Both of the leading securities exchanges in the United States have endorsed the futures product. The American Stock Exchange was first to come forward with its organization of a subsidiary to trade futures in financial instruments. Quickly following was the prestigious New York Stock Exchange's multi-million dollar budget and a separate organization to offer trading in interest rate futures and foreign currencies. It would seem that futures, which may one day include contracts in stock averages as originally proposed by the Kansas City Board of Trade, have arrived and are here to stay.

All the foregoing notwithstanding, it is patent that commodity futures trading is not an easy out for either hedger or speculator, and hardly suitable for the uninitiated and underfinanced. But neither is the ownership of four cars, three houses, and gold-plated water faucets. Still, some persons do boast such affluence. And more persons and many more businesses than you think may be sufficiently positioned in experience and finance to undertake the commodity venture.

For this sophisticated segment of the world's population and business community, commodity futures offer proper risks and rewards. Futures can furnish suitable investor/speculators with limited protection against inflation and, in some cases, against deflation. As noted above, business can take advantage of risk transference. Fair-price discovery is generally advantageous to the public, whether or not they actually trade the futures markets. And many economists maintain that the lack of the futures mechanism in the marketing system would quickly, directly, and adversely affect the consuming public. Since few economic institutions are born, grow and flourish unless they are needed, commodity futures have become a pragmatic part of the free-enterprise system. Its proper expansion will hinge on restrained industry/government regulation, on wise usage by business and public, and ongoing education like that represented by this collection.

The authors you will read in the following pages make significant contributions to advanced commodity thinking. Thus this foreword has been written by one convinced that the commodity cash and futures institution is a growth force too powerful to permit serious players of the economic game the luxury of ignorance as to its workings, influence, and promise.

HOUSTON A. COX, JR.
First Vice President
Smith Barney, Harris Upham & Co., Inc.
New York, New York

ACKNOWLEDGMENTS

This book has its origin in the Symposium on Technical Analysis in Commodities held in New York in October 1978. Both the motivation and perseverance of Dan Reddington of Internatio, Inc. were responsible for its success. My thanks to Dan for his continued help.

When it is all over, the effort involved in organizing and conducting a symposium seems to be forgotten, but the many difficult weeks were overcome by the marketing and administration of Lee and Joy Rose, who took time away from their publications, *Futures Industry Newsletter* and *Managed Account Reports*.

Although not all the speakers are represented here, I would like to express my appreciation to all participants for their excellent work: Ted Hartley, J. Welles Wilder, Jr., Gary Ginter, Joe Ritchie, and Philip Gotthelf. To Todd Lofton I owe a personal thanks for his efforts in moderating the symposium and for his generous help in reviewing and editing the articles in this book as well as writing parts of the introductory material.

Of most importance to me is the continued help and support of my research and ideas by Fred Horn of Bache Halsey Stuart Shields, Inc. Without his encouragement much of my work would be far short of where it is today. The use of Bache's facilities and equipment and the daily help of Mac Fellman, Bob Morford, Bob Keck, and Leon Kaliski were all indispensable.

P. J. K.

CONTENTS

PART 1

BACKGROUND

Perry J. Kaufman has been devoted to commodity research since 1972 when he reoriented his computer service bureau towards the study of price movement in commodities. Since then he has published two other books, Commodity Trading Systems and Methods *(John Wiley & Sons, New York, 1978) and* Point and Figure Commodity Trading Techniques *(Investors Intelligence, Larchmont, N.Y., 1975). He has had many articles appear in* Commodities Magazine, *covering topics from random walk and portfolio distribution to new systems techniques.*

Mr. Kaufman has been actively involved in the study of hedging models for large commercial users of commodities. He is especially interested in the work encompassed by the article "Commodity Selling Model—A Theory of Price Distribution" appearing in this volume. Before moving to New York in 1978 Mr. Kaufman operated a firm on a farm in central Illinois, advising producers on the hedging and sale of their crops.

Perry Kaufman's background has been primarily scientific, including mathematics, astronomy and numerical analysis, receiving degrees at the University of Wisconsin and the University of Southern California. He has taught at the California State University at Northridge and is a member of the Director's Committee of the Columbia University Center for the Study of Futures Markets.

INTRODUCTION

PERRY J. KAUFMAN

There are a few points that must be covered before proceeding with these current topics in commodity technical analysis. The most important is one of perspective. Commodity technical analysis is not voodoo. It is simply a form of price forecasting. Its analysis of trends and patterns is similar to methods used in business for sales projections and seasonality. The severe fluctuations in price which are often found in commodity markets are not unique to it. What makes the problem of analysis so critical is the imposition of high leverage in commodity markets.

We could change the concept of commodity speculating to one of investing by foregoing the use of low margin requirements of the futures markets. Consider how a conservative investment—a pension fund for example—would have performed if it had placed its money in a well diversified commodity portfolio using at least 50% margin instead of the available 5%. During the past 11 years the Consumer Price Index has doubled, from its base of 100 in 1967 to about 200 in 1978. In the same period the Dow Jones Industrial Average moved from 905 to 831, representing a loss of 8% or 16% using 50% margin. The Commodity Research Bureau Futures Price Index gained during 1967–1978, realizing a growth of 400% on 50% margin.

Commodity prices are a true representation of inflation. Although they do not embrace all the elements of the Consumer Price Index, they do contain the foods, fibers, metals, and building materials. Since the introduction of interest rates futures and foreign currencies, a balanced futures portfolio is very nearly representative of our entire economy. When the high leverage is ignored and conservation of capital is no longer a consideration, investments in commodity markets can return more on invested capital than most other investment media.

But most of the analysis in commodities assumes the highest available leverage as a constraint. It therefore makes profits and losses dependent on smaller fluctuations of price movement, and reduces the possibility of basing success on the long-term trend (inflation), the industrial or production cycle, or the seasonality of each commodity. Analysis of commodity prices must therefore be oriented toward risk/reward, profit objectives, and subcycles for individual trades; it is frequently forced into a form of conservation of capital. Management of investment risks becomes as important to success of the system as the method of decision making in trading.

Types of Technical Analysis

Commodity technical analysis can be considered as two major areas of study: concurrent analysis and predictive determination. The predictive method attempts to forecast the extent of price movement over a future time period; for example, wheat will continue higher from August through December, or it will move from $3.50 per bushel to $4.00 per bushel. Both price and time are used in predictive analysis.

Concurrent analysis is also called "autoregressive." It is a determination of the direction of the price at the moment of decision and may be one of only three states: up, down, or sideways. As with the predictive method, concurrent analysis depends on the interval selected; for example, prices can be moving higher in the near term but lower overall. Concurrent analysis incorporates the flexibility of daily change. Each successive autoregressive analysis may result in a changing trend direction, which may cause a new market action or strategy to be taken.

Most systems used in commodity trading are autoregressive. The most well known is the moving average. To take a simple example, when prices cross the average moving up we may consider it a signal of a new upward trend; it remains upward until prices penetrate the moving average going down. Although it is rarely used alone, the moving-average system may determine long-term direction (most often in securities); it may also cause the short-term trend to be redefined daily. It is not intended to predict the extent of the trend in time or value. Breakout systems such as point-and-figure and swing techniques also qualify as autoregressive. They define the current trends and assume a continuation of a trend until a contrary signal occurs.

Predictive methods include the use of price objectives in any form, most commonly those based on seasonality or cyclic phenomena. A simple chart analysis of price objectives may not require a time interval; reaching a support or resistance line on a bar chart may occur either quickly or over a long interval. It should also be noted that a point-and-figure vertical or horizontal count does not indicate time at all. The use of seasonality emphasizes time and not price. For example, fall harvest feedgrain prices often peak during the summer, when weather is an important factor. This allows long hedging positions entered at harvest to be partially lifted in the spring, during or immediately preceding planting, with the balance to be lifted in the summer when the growing conditions may jeopardize production.

Cycles generally combine both time and price. Some techniques consider fluctuations about a normal value, with equal variation of price above and below occurring over a specified interval. Other cycles may be based on the long-term effects of stockpiles and depletion, the size of herds, and the like. Time is the most significant factor for the long-term cycle.

There are three other concerns that must be briefly discussed before entering into the papers themselves. We must first define technical analysis, so that we agree on the limitations of the work. We must also consider the significance of randomness, rather than assume that the price movement of commodities is nonrandom. Lastly, it is necessary to comment on the significance and use of the computer, which is bringing about a new era in virtually every field.

Technical Analysis—What Is It?

In our society of rapid change and scientific advancement we find that terminology which was appropriate yesterday may no longer be exactly correct. Those intensely involved with an area of study or development will introduce additional, more precise terminology to cover new ideas; in the process older terms may become vague generalizations that are occasionally even wrong in their meanings. The term "technical analysis" is now in the category of being too general. It is being used by different groups of analysts with specific but unique meaning to each.

No one will quibble with the word "analysis." Its change in meaning has been very slight and is of lesser importance to us. Comparing the definitions in Webster's Dictionary, 1882 edition (WD) with the 1967 Random House Dictionary (RH) we see similarities in both the general and mathematical definitions.

analysis (WD)

1. A resolution of anything, whether an object of the senses, or of the intellect, into its constituent or original elements . . . .
2. (d) (logic) The tracing of things to their source . . . .
   (e) (math) The resolving of problems by reducing them to equations

analysis (RH)

1. The separating of any material or abstract entity into its constituent elements.
4. (a) (math) An investigation based on the properties of numbers.

We can conclude that analysis of commodities deals with numbers and serves to break these numbers down into their component parts with the use of well-defined methods or rules.

The meaning of the word "technical," however, has moved from general to very specific.

technical (wd)

1. Of, or pertaining to, the useful or mechanical arts; also, to any science, business, or the like; as *technical* phrases; . . . .

technical (rh)

1. Belonging to or pertaining to an art, science, or the like.
3. Using terminology or treating a subject matter in a manner peculiar to a particular field.
7. Noting a market in which prices are determined largely by supply and demand and other such internal factors rather than by general business, economic, or psychological factors that influence market activity: *technical weakness or strength.*

Who would have expected a dictionary, especially in 1967, to be that specific? Even so, the definition is not quite the way "technicians" are currently using the word. Commodity technical analysis is now intended to distinguish the analysis and forecasting of price movement using prices, volume, and open interest from evaluations based on other supply-and-demand statistics. Both methods require a rigid plan and both use numbers and formulas, but the "fundamental" analyst is generally thought to be an economist or someone with related economic interests. The technician can be a chartist, mathematician, engineer, or behaviorist who is applying any combination of standard or innovative methods to analysis of prices, including trendlines, pattern recognition, time-series analysis, and probability. The fundamentalist measures the relationship of price to supply-demand situations. His (or her) tools often include regression analysis based on crop production, finances, import and export factors, and other considerations.

We then define:

Commodity technical analysis—An investigation into the properties of commodity price movement, using prices, volume and open interest, by application of specific, well-defined rules or equations.

Price Movement — The Importance of Its Being Random

The nature of commodity price movement has often been discussed in terms of being "random" or "nonrandom," each containing important implications as to whether the forecasting of commodity price direction is possible. There are many mathematical discussions available. A good collection of references appears in Teweles, Harlow, and Stone, *The Commodity Futures Game, Who Wins? Who Loses? Why?* (McGraw-Hill 1974) within the bibliography under "Price Behavior." The most well-known individual studies are by Holbrook Working, Paul Cootner, Hendrik Houthaker, and A. B. Larson. Rather than discuss the mathematics of the problem, we now look at the implications of different conclusions.

When a series of numbers is called "random" it means that the values, or changes in value, of successive elements in that series contain no predictive information. It says that the fact that today's price was higher or lower than yesterday's does not help in deciding whether tomorrow's price will be higher or lower than today's.

At first glance this statement seems disastrous. It seems to imply that you cannot use prices to forecast the direction of movement. But random-movement studies are phrased differently. They state that a *series* of commodity prices, taken daily over a long interval, are not significantly different from a series of random numbers. It says nothing of the distribution within the interval; it says nothing of the results of combining price movement with other factors or of using other than individual, continuous prices; it says nothing about the ability to profit from that movement.

Studies in random-price movement are not intended to discredit long-term trends. The effects of inflation and seasonality exist in markets. They can be identified and approximated by moving averages and other trending techniques. The existence of these patterns is not contradicted by the "random-walk" theory because they are long-term phenomena based on a combination of elements taken together. Random-motion studies do not say that more than one price, taken together, have no predictive ability.

The distribution of prices over a specific interval could be of great importance to an analysis. If a two-year test had six-month cycles (the grains market, for example) in which prices were biased upward for the first six months then downward for the next six, repeating annually, a study might show the overall price series to be random. In actuality, there were alternating six-month trends. If we had measured the differences between successive prices and compared them against a random distribution, they may have varied by at most the net amount of inflation over the total time interval.

Prices take on added significance when combined with the seasonality of the commodity. If we decompose a series of commodity prices by extracting the seasonal trend, the long-term inflationary bias, and the industrial cycle, we are left with a short-term fluctuation that is expected to be random. Of course, to do this we have taken out three nonrandom factors. There is increasing interest in finding tendencies with this remaining "noise" to show that there are subcycles and patterns unique to this short-term distortion. One such method is discussed in this book as "The Box–Jenkins Approach to Commodity Forecasts."

Prices may also be highly correlated with certain days of the week. If we see prices higher on Monday, lower on Tuesday and Wednesday, and higher again on Thursday and Friday, we have short runs in one direction corresponding to random distribution, but we may have a high correlation of those runs beginning or ending on specific days of the week. Price patterns that continue over a weekend or relate to holidays may be obvious to the trader but transparent to a random-walk student.

The theories of random-price movement imply that there is no correlation over the long term between successive prices. This concept will restrict some analysis, but only in a narrow area. It does not mean that other methods of analysis will not be successful.

Problems with the Current Use of the Computer

The advancement in computer technology within the past 10 years has been spectacular. You can now even carry small computers disguised as calculators. They have capabilities comparable to some of the older full-size computers: 1000-character memory, magnetic card reader, program modules, and other special features. Desktop computers for the home have large memories, cathode ray displays, floppy disks, and other characteristics similar to their larger counterparts; the selection of manufacturers is growing regularly. But the *use* of the computer is slower to change than its technology.

When large-scale computers were introduced to replace older models, they invariably contained a design feature allowing the user to simulate the machine that was being replaced. In effect, you could make a larger, faster, more powerful and expensive machine act just like the smaller, cheaper one! The applications now being implemented on most computers are also the old, well-worn ideas.

The most common use of a computer is to simulate a manual process with greater speed and accuracy. Commodity trading using a computer has largely been used for validation—an unimaginative and wasteful use of the sophistication and power of the computer. Consider the most common application of computer analysis: the moving average. The speed of the equipment has allowed the user to calculate more moving averages on more contracts faster. Tests can be run on different speeds of averages for lengthy historic periods to determine relative effectiveness. And the results may be worthwhile; the user may find a moving average that has worked or will work.

Another computer application may simulate charting. Tests can tell you the best size for a point-and-figure box or the significant penetration of a breakout of the prior week's high or low price. The methods requested of the computer for evaluation all have something in common: they were performed manually before the use of a computer became practical. That is using a new computer to simulate an old one.

Computers can open up an area of analysis not possible in the past. You can evaluate the probability of extreme price moves, the nature of the distribution or variation of prices around a trend, the changes in speed at different price levels, the characteristics of bull and bear markets, and countless applications of probability and statistics. These techniques may be hard to visualize. Probable movement about a trend within a fixed interval is not as comfortable to deal with as a trendline or a new high or low which can be seen on a chart. But that makes the goals more enticing.

Many ultramathematical methods are discounted by traders as unrealistic because they do not represent or simulate actual market phenomena. The "probability" of a new high price is not as valid as a test or penetration of a prior high price. The analyst who takes this approach is reducing a powerful tool to a simple mirror.

Ted Hartley is a Renaissance man. *A holder of graduate degrees in finance and labor management from Pepperdine and Harvard, he is an ex-Naval aviator, a producer and writer of his own television shows and feature films, and a visiting lecturer at Harvard Business School on the subject of using the futures markets and forward contracting as a part of complete corporate strategy. He has been a highly successful practitioner of the commodity markets for ten years, with particular emphasis on the application of computer technology to a better understanding of price behavior. Mr. Hartley currently serves as a consultant to individuals and businesses who require interpretation and planning for comprehensive and coordinated use of the expanding role commodities markets as a business management function.*

The age of electronics and computers has affected everyone. Only a few years ago Victor Comptometer held the calculator market with a monstrous machine with hundreds of buttons. Now a retail store may give away pocket calculators of equal power with only a small purchase. The IBM computers of the early 1960s can be replaced by a Texas Instruments TI59 pocket computer or tenfold by the new Radio Shack computer. You can use a portable terminal the size of a briefcase to call a gigantic computer in some remote part of the United States via a data network, just by using a local telephone number. You can have unlimited calculation power and pay only for what you use.

Will this have any effect on the commodities markets or on price forecasting and analysis? Since many parts of our lives are becoming touched by automation, it is only reason-

able to assume that the commodities markets are not immune. Although past applications and systems may have been primitive or have had varying degrees of success or failure, it is only a matter of time until computerization is an inseparable part of market analysis.   Ted Hartley discusses the evolution of computers and the commodity industry itself. He looks at the problem philosophically, in his own personal way.

This article, "Commodities, Computers and People," has been edited from Mr. Hartley's presentation at the Technical Analysis in Commodities Symposium, *held at the Hotel Pierre in New York on October 18, 1978.   Unlike the other articles in this book, this one has been left in the form of a speech, because of the character of Mr. Hartley's presentation: informative, and at the same time light-hearted and interactive.*

COMMODITIES, COMPUTERS AND PEOPLE

THEODORE R. HARTLEY

How many in this room consider themselves hedgers? Six or seven. How many consider themselves speculative traders? (Large show of hands.) That's the big majority. What are the rest of you? Writers, probably. So the group is primarily speculative in nature, with a sprinkling of 10 people who make their business in journalism.

Roger Gray, one of the great grey-haired minds in the business whom some of you know of from the Food Research Institute at Stanford University, said the other day—referring to the famous cigarette commercial—"the commodity business has come a long way, baby." What he meant was that as recently as the late 1960s, when I was just beginning to get out of the airplanes and into the commodity business, a lot of the things that we are talking about now would not have been understood by the most advanced people in the industry. At that time— if you can put yourself back into the late 1960s—can you imagine the New York Stock Exchange inviting the Commodity Exchange to join together and form a very important organization? See where this whole business has come.

There are some interesting statistics about that, in passing: during the late 1960s there were said to be about 20 important pool operators of commodity funds in the United States.   Now, of those who are registered—and some people don't, I understand—the total number had risen to about 227 by 1975.   And last year it rose to about 482. That means that 482 people have stepped up to play it safe about managing money and have registered with the government.   Four hundred eighty-two people managing money seems like a lot more than the 20 whom we knew less than 10 years ago, and I suspect there are others who have not registered.   Advisors, which is sometimes another hat worn by pool operators, have risen from about 100 who were registered with the CEA to 219 in 1975; now there are about 728 of them, and the CFTC (Commodity Futures Trading Commission) says that they get about two registrations a day. The point is that it's a big business; the fact that there are so many important people who are here today also supports that.   The fact that you pay this outrageous fee to come in and hear Perry Kaufman and all of us shows how much money there is in the business.

I am going to make some assumptions in talking. I am going to run briefly through the point at which the commodity business got into the computer business and discuss a little about what that is like, what people are doing with it, and—a window that some of you have looked through probably more closely than I—where it is going and what it will be like 3 or 4 years from now.   I am making an assumption I hope you will share with me, one which has already been referred to: that, completely in opposition to Dr. Paul Cootner's famous treatise on the randomness of stock prices, sequential dependence of commodity prices does exist. There is some logical relationship between sequential prices in some time continuums.   There are trends and there are repetitive patterns. People make rules based on that sequential dependence, and there are many kinds of rules.

For example, a single rule can exist under a system, although generally a system consists of the application of more than one rule.   But you can operate with a single rule—for example, Thorpe, who wrote *Beat the Dealer*, has a rule which he says works 90% of the time; the rule is, if the home team is the 11-point underdog, always bet on them.   That is the kind of rule which can be applied to the commodities markets; for example, if the nearby expiring wheat contract is at a discount to the next deferred contract, always buy the near, sell the next, and follow the two to expiration and the nearby contract.

There are a series of rules similar to that which we have all used, and some of them we know consciously and some we know unconsciously. They are not systems, but they do exist and support my other assumption that basically all markets have a psychological underpinning. This underlying pattern can come from emotions of people rather than from what may be reality. At a Harvard seminar somebody asked me the question, "What is the commodity market and what makes it move?" I struggled to break it down into parts without much clarity. Later I developed the short functional description: commodity markets serve to net out the emotional reactions of people to varying degrees of imagined scarcity.

Now what kind of scarcity are we talking about? (It is interesting to notice that people are emotional: imagine these words used in a business conceived as being technical and analytical in nature.) The scarcity can relate to opportunity, to money, or to the commodity itself. The point is that people tend to work from varying degrees of imagined scarcity or surplus. I picked out Gerald Loeb, one of the great early writers about prices and price movements. He wrote *The Battle for Investment Survival*, which is still one of my four bibles. He mentioned in there—he is often considered a fundamentalist in some ways—that "the most important single factor in shaping the security markets was the public psychology. It's the reason why I'm not particularly impressed with academic calculation purporting to show what this or that stock is worth nowadays involving complicated calculations often worked out on the computer." He goes on to point out that ultimately, making a practical application, psychologists should be better traders than a computer technician, because a psychologist will be able to relate to what is going on in the public mind. And that takes me to my second bible.

Psychology of Trading

How many of you have read *Reminiscences of a Stock Operator*? That is a good third of the room. Those of you who have not should get a copy if you want to find out how the market was in the good-old-days, which we will talk about in a minute. I just want to share with you one of the most exciting things, one of the things that turned me on to the commodity market, although it was written about the stock market. This is Jesse Livermore, who was one of the great speculators, who made several fortunes in his lifetime and ended up committing suicide because he said that as a result of government interference and regulation there was really no excitement left. He had decided that the excitement was what he really wanted. He talked about once when he was broke, and he came into town, hitchhiking his way from Florida, and was sitting in a trading room, watching the tickertape. He said "By reasons of conditions known to the whole world, the stock that was most bullish in those critical days of early 1915 was Bethlehem Steel." He says, "I think I told you it has been my experience that *whenever a stock crosses 100 or 200 or 300 for the first time, it nearly always keeps going for 30 or 50 points—and after 300, faster than after 100 or 200.*" See the beginning of a system of rules? How many of you believe that soybeans will move more when they go through $6 than when they go through $5.91? Does anyone believe that even numbers or zeroes make any difference?

As a matter of fact, acording to Livermore, it's n old trading principle. He said, and I quote loosely, "I was so eager to begin that I could not think of anything else; but I held myself in leash. I saw Bethlehem Steel climb, every day, higher and higher, as I was sure it would. . . . Every point the stock went up meant five hundred dollars that I had not made." This is from a guy who is broke. "But I sat tight and instead of listening to my loud-mouthed hopes or to my clamorous beliefs. I heeded only the level voice of my experience and the counsel of common sense. Once I had a decent stake together I could afford to take chances." That, by the way, is the common fault of a lot of commodity traders: Once I have a stake together, I can afford to take chances, and when I'm broke I can't and that's when I make the money and when I lose it I can't afford to take chances. . . . He goes on, "Without a stake, taking chances, even slight chances, was a luxury utterly beyond my reach. . . . I really began to waver and sweat blood when the stock got up to 90. Think of what I had not made by not buying, when I was so bullish. Well, when it got to 98 and I said to myself, 'Bethlehem is going through 100 and when it does the roof is going to blow clean off!' The tape said the same thing more than plainly. In fact, it used a megaphone. I tell you, I saw *100* on the tape and the ticker was only printing *98*. And I knew that wasn't the voice of my hope or the sight of my desire, but the assertion of my tape-reading instinct. So I said to myself, 'I can't wait until it goes through 100. I have to get it now. It's as good as gone through par.' I rushed away to my broker's office and put in an order to buy five hundred shares of Bethlehem Steel. The market was then 98. I got five hundred shares at 98 to 99, and after that she shot right up, and closed that night, I think, at 114 or 115. I bought five hundred shares more. The next day Bethlehem Steel was 145."

Those of you who had the fun of being in a major bull market, buying something and seeing it go, know what Livermore is talking about; and those kinds of plays are going to exist for the intuitive speculators. One of the things about being an intuitive speculator is that you probably win bigger, lose more trades and you may also have more fun than working with computer tapes.

After Livermore, in looking again at the development of systems, we must mention Graham and Dougherty, who first started developing systems of security analysis. Donchian, of course, is especially famous in that area; another who came up in the 1950s and 1960s, who may not be known to you, is named Amos Hostetter—a trader in New Jersey.

Hoffstetter is a good example of the way people used to work before there were computers. He had three basic tenets, in addition to the non-randomness of the market. One was that markets do trend and that the trends should be identified first. The second was the existence of support/resistance levels, and the third was the recognition of patterns. These were the three things on which he developed his system, and they are actually not far from the computer systems we are going to look at briefly. The important point is that Hoffstetter did it all by hand. He would say you can only watch two or three commodities at a time, or you can only watch two or three options, and those were the practical limits. Therefore, the system you were using would be all done by your own hand unless you had a lot of help out back who were generating a lot of work. As technical analysis worked into the computer age, some strange things began happening in the market.

There are a few charts that show the difference between where we were in those early days and where we are now . . . I have seen this chart 100 times, and it is always fascinating to look at (Figure 1). You can see the low prices along the bottom—from 1969. And that carries on back into the 1950s without very much change. It points out what Morgan Maxfield stated, that the good old days really are gone forever. Those days of $6\frac{1}{2}\%$ discount interest rate and $\frac{1}{2}\%$ a year inflation are gone, and they are not going to come back again—and neither are those markets. For a period of 50 years you had relatively compressed markets in terms of what came later. The other thing that made most commodity traders right in the early days, the precomputer days, is the general upward bias running over 50 years, which is slightly ahead of the $\frac{1}{2}\%$ annual inflation rate. Going into the computer age in commodities seems to coincide pretty well with the way the chart takes off in late 1972, followed by the changes that we can note.

SOYBEANS

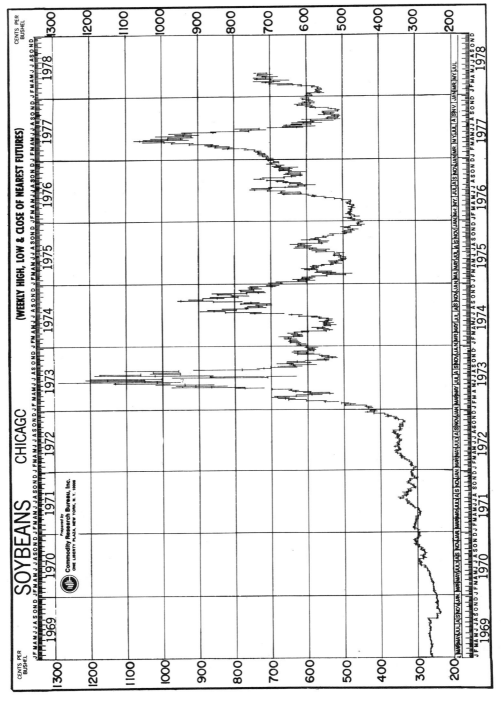

FIGURE 1
Soybean price history.

18

In the 1950s I came from the Midwest, and I remember talking to a farmer just outside Des Moines who was trying to keep track of hog prices in Omaha. He had worked out elaborate arrangements using pay telephones so that he could find out pretty closely what the hog prices were from moment to moment in Omaha. And that affected the price of his corn and what he did with his crops in Des Moines. There was a relationship.

In this era as we are fully developing into the computer age we have that same relationship with Japan, Russia, and China. They have a similar effect on silver prices or cocoa prices in New York as hog prices in Omaha have to corn in Des Moines. I was recently talking about a novel concerning an American bureaucrat who decides he is going to make his millions by announcing a big purchase of corn and wheat in China and then simultaneously cancelling it once he is short the market.

The point is that the interrelationships of the world are part of the reason for the changing price patterns; it is one of the reasons we are never going to go back to the old days. Daniel Seligman—who runs a company called Benchmark in southern California and, I think, does the best work on financials and interest rate instruments—points out that over the next 2 years the inflation rate—the real inflation rate—is going to be about 10%. Using normal statistical projections over the next year it is going to run somewhere between $8\frac{1}{2}\%$ and 14%. That is, $8\frac{1}{2}\%$ if we really clamp down and 14% if we continue to expand at our present rate. It is therefore probably 10%, or a little above, a rate that can be projected out for some period of time. No matter what our concerns, those are the kind of growth rates that we are talking about: somewhere between $8\frac{1}{2}\%$ and 14%. We are not going to have charts as in the 1950s and 1960s with the old inflation rate. Gary Ginter has pointed out that his correlations on volatility didn't work if you omitted that rate of inflation; in fact, you wouldn't get a correlation at all. All of this leads up to the fact that the markets as we used to know them—nice, calm things where gentlemen could trade and be nice to each other—are gone forever.

And just in time the computers arrived, because otherwise the computers in our heads would never be able to handle it. Where most of the systems before had two, three, or four rules and carried 4 or 5 years of data written down on a piece of paper, now if there is data available (and we have talked a little bit about how difficult it is to get data) you can run systems back indefinitely and cover all options and all commodities that are traded in the world. Ultimately, the decisions about how you are going to run your business—using speculating or hedging —amount to decisions of whether to buy, and what and when, at what price and how much; you are now able to make these decisions largely based on the discipline a computer provides. So let's go back and look at it from the point of view of the ten people in the audience concerned with hedging, which is a point of view which I often take. What are the problems of bringing all this hardware and all this software to bear as part of corporate policy? That is really what you want to do as a hedger.

Risks and Rewards

How many of you believe that the hedging function in a corporation should make money? Should a hedging operation make money as a separate part of a corporation? How many of you believe that the function of the hedging section of the corporation is basically to protect the manufacturing profit? There seems to be about an even split. Some people who are hedgers are really sophisticated speculators; for example, you may have a company called Hedging, Inc. which is really just taking advantage of the market fluctuations. Then there are some people who call themselves hedgers who say "We're not going to make profits or losses on the raw materials end of it, but what we're going to do is protect the manufacturer's profit, which is where we make our money." That kind of a difference is the basis of the problems of consultants who are trying to decide how to wrap a hedging policy around corporate policy. How do you deal with a chairman of the board who says, "Yeah, we want to protect our manufacturing profit, but how come the hedging section is losing money?"

The comparison goes all the way from one end, as Lee Richartz in California who defines the complete hedge as covering the *banker's risk*, which means you seek out every risk there is—interest rates, raw materials, currencies, labor transportation—and you hedge them all. According to his terminology, if you haven't hedged every risk there is, you are not a hedger. That's what I call a *banker's risk* or *banker's hedging*.

And what are your rewards for hedging? It certainly isn't a successful profit-and-loss statement in the hedging section of your corporate annual report. What it does, if the banker understands this, is to allow him to lend more money than a standard banking situation permits. You might recall the H. P. Hood case—that's an orange juice and milk company in Boston that decided in the early 1970s that they should be hedging. So they went and picked out a nice, bright Harvard Business School graduate, started a hedging operation in which he would buy orange juice whenever everyone said it was low and sell when it was high. That year, which I believe was 1971, he had just entered the market in November by deciding that he was going to buy concentrate from the futures market and then sell it into the cash market from the point of high demand in February and March. Then there was a freeze in January. At that time Hood had very large production, the warehouse was relatively full, and he was low in the futures market, all at the same time. So that year they made money on their orange juice production, and they made about a million dollars on their hedging operation. The chairman of the board thought that was really great, but he also didn't understand how it happened. So he asked the Harvard Business School graduate to explain exactly how this hedging thing worked. The graduate said that it was the same question asked of Will Rogers, which was "How do you make money in the stock market?" Will Rogers answered, "Well, what you do is you buy. You look at some stocks that are going up and you buy the stocks that are going up and," he said, "if they don't go up, you don't buy them." It's the same way with those hedging operations.

It inevitably happened that they tried to repeat it the next year, by going long in the futures market as well as long in concentrate. There was a big freeze, repetitive cycles fell off in January, and they lost about a million dollars; then everybody was asking what it's all about. H. P. Hood has since been taken over by another organization, and this other organization is getting a rather sophisticated hedging system which has nothing to do with whether the price is high or low—which is the risk approach of true hedgers. The tendency to speculate is so thoroughly engrained in each one of us—hedgers and speculators alike—that without some kind of discipline, either imposed rigidly by ourselves or through computers, it is very hard to be consistent in trading.

Essential Discipline

One of the important things the computer age has done is to offer a way of preventing the Livermores of the world from going into the market while watching the tape that says 98 and reading it as 100. It gives precise points at which you are going to enter and precise criteria with which you're going to get out. It permits the development of a well-defined hedging policy, whether it is a banker's hedger or a speculative hedger. Compared to the banker's hedge, an aggressive businessman may view risk as speculative opportunity and may at times sell an inventory of raw materials in the futures market, when the futures market will pay more for it than the manufacturers or dealers would pay. At times he may not be hedged at all and find that the best thing to be done is to figure up the price of your inventory and then take the other side of businessman's risk hedge, which will require trading sections in the companies that are involved in raw materials. That application will be an exciting area in which to operate with the use of the computer techniques you are hearing about today. By the way, I was talking to a fellow while riding in a plane, and he was saying that the company he represents makes loans to business and, he said, since you can't always make the businessman who will receive the loans understand hedging, that the Foothill Group, a loan company, is now setting up a small division to hedge the raw materials purchased through the loan and to be sure the company's inventory value doesn't deteriorate during the life of the loan. The reward for using effective hedging programs should be that you are able to borrow more money at a lower interest rate. But this is not yet a reality, since hedging is not a clear-cut operation like buying and selling.

The Computer in Commodities

What happened to speculators and hedgers who have come into the computer age, and what is the difference between using computers and the "old days" when you used to be able to do it on paper? One of the things that has happened is phenomenal; it is a mind-boggling expansion of the use of computers. Consider the cost of computer equipment over the past few years. The price of computer hardware has decreased dramatically. For $5000 you can now buy a computer that will fit on a desk top and will do something that only 10 years ago would have cost you more than $1,000,000 and would have taken a much larger space. The availability of a large, inexpensive and reliable computer memory is one of the things that has allowed the commodity market to get much more complicated; at the same time it has caused the expansion of the number of traders and advisors.

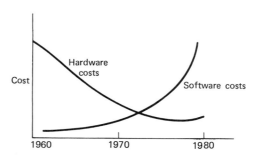

FIGURE 2
Computer costs.

While computers become more complex and the memory capabilities increase, the cost of software has increased. It is more difficult to get computer programs. A good systems analyst can make significant contributions to the commodity market. As those of you who are in the computer business know, the problem is not so much where to get your hardware or how you get the money for your hardware, but how you develop a system and how much are you going to pay for it to keep it competitive. The phenomenon that you are experiencing now is that the software is a bigger financial component of the overall system than the computer is itself, and that direction will continue.

If you picture a chart of software and hardware costs, you can get something like Figure 2, where software costs are climbing sharply and hardware costs are declining at a slower rate. Interestingly enough, most of the components for the hardware come from outside the United States; with the fluctuation of the currency price rates, the decrease of the value of the dollar has caused an upturn in hardware costs, so that you will find as the yen gets dearer and dearer against the dollar, you'll find less and less of a decrease in computer prices.

Gearing Up for a System—The Data

When you consider using a computer now there are two big problems. One is the data base. Dunn & Hargitt made a data base available for the first time in about 1972, and that seems to have been the basis for most historic data bases. And everybody I know in the computer business has spent a big part of their time cleaning that data up, and it is still a problem. It is important to ask yourself, "How do you get data that has enough validity to use to develop theories and test out systems?" Helmut Weymar, who wrote a book on the dynamics of the cocoa market (which may be the definitive book on the cocoa market and really worth reading if you are interested in technical systems), said that in order to develop his very complicated cocoa system, he spent $600,000 gathering and cleaning data.

It is Weymar's theory, and one of mine as well, that all data and all prices as far back as 80 years ago are valuable. People still react the same way to falling or to increased prices today as they did that long ago, and therefore whatever reliable price data you can get will be useful; if you don't have that data, then you are missing some data you really need to validate whatever it is that you are doing. Weymar spent all that money going back and digging out of old London newspaper articles—the daily highs and lows and midpoints of the cocoa market. If you are going into technical systems, that is one of the things you are going to have to face. It is going to be hard to get good historic price data, and it is going to be expensive when you get it, and it will have to be checked all the time. Whatever you can buy on the street should be expected to have, perhaps, a 4 to 5% error, in my experience. And so the first thing you are going to have to deal with is the time and effort necessary to scrub the data in order to make it useful. But the data certainly is valuable, and I do not feel that you can afford to be without it if you are going to have a system that makes sense.

Designing a System

The other thing that must be taken into consideration when developing a system is the heuristic characteristics of it. Should it be self-correcting? As you enter new data and gain experience today, is the system correcting what was previously decided was happening? If you can't design a program that basically corrects itself, your computer software cost is going to continue to mount, and you are going to lose efficiency, considerable efficiency.

Your program is also going to want to look at multidimensionality, where each dimension represents a characteristic of your trading or your hedging philosophy. What are the things you consider important, and how are you going to test them in order to find out how they are important? How do you know that you have thought of everything? There is no excuse when you are developing a computer program not to test every relationship to see whether there is a combination of importance. If you haven't tested thoroughly, then your program is going to be weak in that area, because others are now doing multidimensional programs.

Looking back at Figure 1, the soybean price chart, we can see one of the things that Perry Kaufman was talking about, the rising value of the base price due to inflation. The price lows which follow peak prices keep getting higher.* Even better than soybeans, copper is a clear example of applicability to technical systems. Our experience in copper has been that any kind of a trend-following system would have made money every year since 1969. Copper is one of those commodities for which even a moving average crossover system seems to work relatively well. Now that I have said it, everyone will go out and use it, and it is not going to work anymore.

Interrelationships between commodities are becoming increasingly important and more complex. I have a new theory about currencies, interest rates, and commodities that more than ever makes me feel the world is getting smaller. From the recent currency fluctuations it seems that currencies are acting just like the common stock of publicly traded corporations, for which value goes up and down in relation to the public's view of the corporation's potential profit or loss and the capabilities of its management. The changing curency values, then, relate directly to the level of inflation in each country and the cost of money, which then directly affect all aspects of agricultural production and manufacturing. The important thing to recognize in this example is that there may be a direct relationship among these three large areas: currencies, interest rates, and commodities (and, of course, management).

More and more, as I talk to computer analyst and modeling experts around the country, I find that they are asking questions which might seem as absurd as "What is the price of platinum? How does that relate to the price of corn?" It is important to know that they are not assuming that there is *not* some kind of interrelationship.

M.I.T. has two of the systems which I have seen around the country that I find most exciting; one is called *Sleuth* and the other is called

* See "Price Volatility" article.

Comex. *Sleuth* is basically a situational trader, that is to say, what it does is to develop a pattern of recognition. It goes through the data base, the statistical data base, and finds out how many times that particular pattern has led to a certain result. It then creates situations and propositions such that if, based on a past pattern, you have a price rise of a specific percent magnitude without a decline of a certain percent, you will know the probabilities of the price move continuing beyond the last point. It is an exciting system—a situational, problemistic trading method which is in the forefront of development.

The *Comex* system is basically a chess player. Based on chess-playing models, it considers the market an adversary. It says, "If the market makes a move, what do I do to counter and protect my position?" It plays each situation or position all the way through to the end. It is a very complex program and an exciting one, when viewed as an adversary relationship.

Bill Adamson in Los Angeles is an ex-Hughes Aircraft designer, a ballistics specialist, who developed what we call the *ballistics system.* It basically works like a ballistic missile, in that you develop a situation by pattern recognition and you project the hit point. The farther that price goes through time (the more prices that are used as a basis of projection), the narrower will be the span of the target variation; as new prices develop, you are constantly narrowing down the projection. Any movement of price outside of the narrowing band then changes the ballistic curve, and you project a new objective. The ballistics approach, which is another point of view, must also be considered one of the forerunners of systems analysis.

Someone working with computers in Denver said that brokers have the problem of not understanding orders and of getting them wrong. He is very excited about something which we have all experienced already by receiving computer telephone calls—he is working on a system by which the computer makes actual voice transmissions and relays them to the brokers in written form. Certainly it is within the realm of possibility. If you were going to actually give the order audibly, you would rather record it on tape than have it written down.

Probabilistic systems are essential. It is surprising that probabilistic approaches are not used more. Certainly, you can develop standard bell-shaped curves, and in any type of market you can determine that the odds of a rise to a certain point are 80%, and the chance of a decline to a certain point is 20%.

Keeping Your Perspective

The question is now whether man can really beat the computer or whether he must play with it. The answer is simply to get above the situation and keep in mind what it is you are trying to do with a trading program. To help, I want to tell you about one of the more important books which will influence your commodity trading. It is a lovely little book by Richard Bach, who wrote *Jonathan Livingston Seagull*; it is a book called *Illusions*. It is a very touching book, and it is sound commodity trading because he talks about what it is we do from our own point of view. At one end of one chapter he points out the following, which I think is worth remembering when you are studying computer programming:

> A cloud does not know why it moves in such a direction at such a speed [and you can say that the price of corn does not know why it moves in such a direction at such a speed]. It just feels a compulsions that this is the place to go now. But the sky knows the reasons and the patterns behind those movements and you'll know, too, if you lift yourself high enough above to see beyond the horizon.

That is what we want to do with computer science and what you want to do with your program. Get yourself far enough above the movements and directions of prices so you can develop some sound strategy.

THE EXPANDING VIEW OF PRODUCT PRICING

PERRY J. KAUFMAN

Product prices are characterized by the geographic areas in which the product originates. Often these areas are represented by a price-surface schema relating the product cost by location as a function of the regional supply-demand and transportation from the source of production. Since the growing of crops, mining, and so forth are restricted by climate and other physical land requirements, the geography of supply is normally distorted. In the case of agricultural commodities of wide production, such as wheat, corn, and soybeans, the seasonality of the prices is most apparent in the immediate growing areas and more transparent to the buyer as the distance from these areas is increased. The cost of transportation, storage, interest rates, and other normal carrying charges, as well as the risks assumed by the middleman in inventory, cause varying burdens to be added to prices which may tend to deseasonalize the price trends.

The greatest effect on prices outside the production region is competition from other producing areas. A user situated equidistant from two producers, with equal transportation costs, will select the best price, thus forcing a competitive price adjustment between two physically distant regions. The large buyer will always shop for the best price. Until recently, the basic fundamentals of supply-demand were adequate to analyze purchasing opportunities. This brings us to the international market and the effects of shifting currency values on prices.

Naturally, the extent of export-import within a related product range will determine the extent of the effect caused by relative changes in currencies. The calendar year 1978 exhibited an apparently unnatural price movement for most major United States crops. As seen in Figure 1, prices of hard wheat in Kansas City climbed steadily all year. The winter crop harvest season of May and June would normally put pressure on prices once the size of the crop was known. In addition, 1978 was a year of great surplus with no surprises. Large crops were anticipated in most of the world, and expectations were fulfilled. Why did

FIGURE 1
Hard wheat at Kansas City, U.S. $ per 100 bushels

the prices of wheat, soybeans, and other crops increase throughout the year, defying the seasonality and fundamental supply-demand factors?

The reasons can be easily found in the loss of value of the United States dollar. The United States consumer can no longer analyze value in terms of dollars. If the purchaser waited for a seasonal low during harvest, he would still be waiting as prices continue to rise.

Let us consider what the price of these crops appears to be from the eyes of a typical European consumer, by expressing the cost of a bushel of wheat in Deutschemarks (West German marks). Figure 1 shows the price of wheat in United States dollars and clearly indicates a steady rise since mid-1977, despite an increasing supply. Figure 2 is on the same scale as Figure 1, but expresses wheat prices in terms of Deutsche-

FIGURE 2
Wheat in West German marks per bushel.

FIGURE 3
Wheat in ounce of gold per bushel.

marks by division; the price rise from mid-1977 is nearly eliminated. Figure 3, expressed in terms of the spot price of gold, shows that the original increase in wheat prices over the period considered may have actually been a decrease, as we would have expected.

The seasonality of prices, which normally shows depressed levels for U.S. wheat in mid-year, clearly exists in terms of gold; whereas the seasonality is not clear in either United States dollars or Deutschemarks. Is any one standard better than another? By observing the earlier years of the three diagrams more carefully, we see that there is great similarity between the price of wheat expressed in United States dollars and the price in Deutschemarks; there is, however, noticeable variation between both of these and the price of wheat expressed in terms of gold. Note in Figure 3 the sharper decline in early 1974, followed by a sideways pattern through the end of 1976, resulting in a slow price deterioration.

The best selection for the representation of prices must be a unit of measure common to the world economy. The use of a single currency, such as Deutschemarks, may be appropriate for purchases relating directly to that country but is still severely biased by specific local economic factors. A weighted pooling of various currencies based on their corresponding national output may be the best representation of value, but this method is subject to frequent reevaluation because of the constant individual economic changes. Gold appears to be the most convenient common standard of value. Although it does not relate absolutely to any one economy, it relates generally to most economies. When the USSR bought wheat in 1973–1974, it subsequently sold gold to cover the purchase; this past year the United States sold gold to counter the trend of inflation.

Suppose a purchaser is in the market for a large quantity of wheat. By considering only Figure 1 we may conclude that wheat prices are in an uptrend but have potential of going either higher or lower. In fact, wheat prices may go either way, depending on the changing value of the United States dollar alone. In Figure 3 the situation is much clearer. Prices are constant at just over .015 ounces of gold per bushel. If we believe that the supply of wheat is at a peak, then the prices shown here can only go up. If we believe in addition that the United States economy may be stabilizing, then the prices in Figure 3 may go up quickly. In either case, the price of wheat in international terms is low, and a user may find it advantageous to fix the price at this level. This is done by buying wheat and selling gold at the current rate of .015 ounces per bushel.

Since the value of the United States dollar has been inversely related to the price of gold, an increase in the value of the dollar will require more ounces of gold to be spent for the same bushel of wheat. If the value of wheat remains at $3.50 per bushel and the price of gold is at $200 per ounce, Figure 3 will be priced at .0175 ounces per bushel. If gold prices move down to $190 per ounce, the value in Figure 3 goes to .0184. while if United States wheat prices move to $4.00 and gold remains constant at $200, we get the price of .0200 ounces per bushel. For prices to decline further in terms of ounces of gold per bushel, we must have an increase in world supply and a further decline in the value of the United States dollar.

Conclusion

Although the variations in currency value have always been implicit in the price of a commodity with a significant import or export market, the recent severe fluctuations in the United States dollar have magnified their importance. The fundamentals of supply and demand still interact as before, but they are heavily shadowed by currency variations.

Introduction of expanded world trade with China, better communications, and transportation have probably changed the nature of local pricing forever. Even the prices received by a farmer from his local elevator reflect changes in foreign currency values. It is now necessary to reduce United States price quotations to a more common standard and to reevaluate prior fundamental and technical analysis in terms of this new standard. At the present time this seems to be gold.

PART 2

SYSTEMS

Frank Hochheimer, Manager of Technical Analysis and Computer Applications for the Commodity Division of Merrill Lynch, has both preached and practiced. After receiving a master's degree in mathematics from Hofstra University and a master's degree in econometrics from the New School for Social Research, he taught mathematics and economics for eight years at New York Institute of Technology. In 1975 he left the world of academia to join Merrill Lynch as a commodity analyst, where he has developed several computer-based commodity trading models for hedgers and speculators. This combination of theoretical and practical experience is most unusual, and equips him very well to talk objectively about the computerized evaluation of moving averages and other trading strategies.

The two research reports that follow represent the best examples of forethought. Frank Hochheimer has taken the most basic trend identification methods and examined them with a simple clarity that should set an example for other analysts. It is important that we understand the variations of the basic methods before complicating the results by combining other techniques or filters.

The first paper, "Moving Averages," looks at the three most popular trending methods: a simple moving average of equally weighted days, a linear weighting of days, and an exponential smoothing of days. The first method, often called a standard or simple moving average, has been popular in the securities industry for many years and has been accepted by commodity analysts as fundamental to their work. Linear weighted averages represented the first major variation from the standard moving average and became most recently popular with the publication of MPTDI in Commodities *magazine in 1972. Exponential smoothing has constantly gained in popularity, because of its continuity in retaining old data, however discounted. Hochheimer defines and analyzes the performance of each method very well.*

The second report, "Channels and Crossovers," appeared 6 months after the first, and it evaluates several additional trading models. A single moving average may not be a practical indicator for a trading signal, since it offers no latitude for commitment to a new trend. Once entered, it is necessary to stay in the new position until proved right or wrong by a substantial price move in either direction. The channel width, based on a price range or a natural formation of the high and low prices, offers a band of commitment for a new market position and can be related to a risk/reward plan for program management.

The crossover method has also been popular among professionals. It combines two moving averages of different speeds that interact to identify the longer-term trend and the shorter-term timing.

We are grateful to the firm of Merrill Lynch Pierce Fenner & Smith for their permission to reprint these excellent reports [both articles have been edited slightly] but mostly we express our gratitude to them for supporting worthwhile research.

MOVING AVERAGES

An Explanation and Computerized Testing of Simple, Linear, and Exponentially Smoothed Moving Averages

FRANK HOCHHEIMER

Moving averages have long fascinated the commodity speculator. Many variations on the theme have been put forth. It is the purpose of this article to examine three major basic types of moving averages and compare their results over the same testing period. A weighting and ranking approach has been used here to ascertain what we feel are consistently good trend indicators. This article will provide information on simple moving averages, exponentially smoothed moving averages, and linearly weighted moving averages. The period analyzed will be for every contract that traded from January, 1970, through December, 1976, for the commodities shown in Table 1.

It was assumed that each contract was traded from its inception to the last business day prior to expiration month.

Reprinted by permission of Merrill, Lynch Pierce Fenner & Smith.

TABLE 1 COMMODITIES ANALYZED		
Copper	Cocoa	Soybean Meal
Silver	Corn	Soybean Oil
Cotton	Wheat	Pork Bellies
Sugar	Soybeans	Hogs
	Plywood	

Concepts Explained

A moving average is employed to smooth the effects of erratic market behavior. It is a trend-following system that does not do any predicting. The most basic is the *simple moving average*. Each day in the average is weighted equally. In a 5-day average, each day is weighted 20%. In a 25-day average, each day is weighted 4%. A criticism which is often heard is that it is slow to react to dramatic price changes, but, of course, this can also be a benefit. In other words, the oldest day included has as much weight as the latest day in the average. Another criticism is that one does not take into account days beyond the length of the average. To answer the weighting criticism, the *linearly weighted moving average* assigns weight to each price, assigning the heaviest weight to the most recent day and so on, back for the number of days in the average. A 5-day average would assign a weight of 5 to the most recent day, a 4 to the day before that, and so on. The result is then divided by the sum of the weights. But this average still only takes a certain number of days into account. The *exponentially smoothed moving average* takes the entire price history of a contract into account and assigns weights by a mathematical formula. Again, the most recent days are given the most weight. The questions we are trying to answer are: Is there a significant difference in the results obtained between these averages, and which perform the best (give the most consistent results)?

Definitions

Model—Consists of a set of rules that are fixed by mathematical formulas. They do contain some variables that can be adjusted by the user.

Strategy—Within a model, changing any variable leads to a different strategy, for example, a model of a moving average system may have strategies of 3-day, 4-day, 20-day, 50-day moving averages.

Objective

A weighting method was constructed to weight the results of each contract as to cumulative profits, largest string of losses, and the ratio of profits to losses. This was done on each contract simulated for each model and for each strategy within the model tested. By a series of sorting procedures a consistent approach to the market was sought. This simply means that we are not looking for the optimal strategy in each contract individually, but a strategy that will consistently perform well according to our weighting system over time in the model. For comparison with our consistent estimates, the results of the 5, 10, and 20-day simple moving averages, linearly weighted moving averages, and the exponentially smoothed moving averages have been placed in tables at the end of this article. A word of caution is in order here. As with all historical testing procedures, success in the past is in no way a guarantee of success in the future. The results are offered as an informational guide to those speculators and hedgers who use these systems.

Long-Term Objective

We are not only interested in arriving at a consistent indicator for the above commodities using various strategies within a model, but we are also interested in comparing models and indicating which model and strategy works best, that is, comparing the consistent strategies for the hog market using moving averages, exponential smoothing, and so forth.

Simple Moving Average Constraints Defined

1. The moving average (M.A.) of N days closes are calculated including today's close.

$$\text{M.A.} = [\text{Close } (M) + \text{Close } (M-1) + \text{Close } (M-2) + \cdot \cdot \cdot + \text{Close } (M-N+1)]/N$$

where M = today's data (use only business days)
N = number of days

2. If today's close penetrates the moving average on the upside, a buy is placed on the opening tomorrow. If today's close penetrates the moving average on the downside, a sell is placed on the opening tomorrow.

3. The model is always in the market. When a new buy or sell signal is generated, the old position is liquidated simultaneously.

4. If the high and low of the next day are equal, then the assumption is made that the market is locked limit, and a trade cannot be made on that day. The trade will be done on the first day the market is not locked the limit.

Simple Moving Average Results— Consistent Indicators

Table 2 gives the most consistent moving average in Column 1. Column 2 shows the cluster of values that performed well if such a cluster existed. Column 3 shows cumulative net profit for all contracts traded in the 1970–1976 period (defined previously), using current Merrill Lynch commissions and current contract point values. Column 4 indi-

TABLE 2　SIMPLE MOVING AVERAGES—TABLE OF RESULTS

	Best Day	(Best Range)	Cumulative Profits or Losses (Net)	Largest String of Losses	Number Trades	Number Profitable Trades	Number Losing Trades
Cocoa	54	53–59	$ 87,957	$−14,155	600	157	443
Corn	43	43–46	24,646	− 6,537	565	126	439
Sugar	60	55–60	270,402	−15,563	492	99	393
Cotton	57	52–57	68,685	−11,330	641	121	520
Silver	19	—	42,920	−15,285	1,393	429	964
Copper	59	54–59	165,143	− 7,687	432	158	274
Soybeans	55	55–60	222,195	−10,800	728	151	577
Soybean Meal	68	65–70	22,506	−20,900	704	148	556
Wheat	41	40–45	65,806	−12,550	480	124	356
Pork Bellies	19	16–25	97,925	− 9,498	774	281	493
Soybean Oil	69	65–70	89,416	− 8,920	586	122	464
Plywood	68	65–70	1,622	− 3,929	372	98	274
Hogs	16	16–20	35,595	− 7,190	1,093	318	775

cates the largest string of losses in any one contract not including margin money. Column 5, 6, and 7 show total number of trades, total number of profitable trades, and total number of losing trades, respectively, for all contracts traded in the test period.

Exponentially Smoothed Moving Average
Constraints Defined

1. The exponentially smoothed moving average (E.S.M.A.) is calculated including today's close.

$$\text{E.S.M.A.} = K\text{Close}(M) + K(1-K)\text{Close}(M-1) + K(1-K)^2\text{Close}(M-2) + \cdots$$

where $K = 2/(N + 1)$, defined as a smoothing constant
$M =$ today's data (use only business days)
$N =$ number of days

2. If today's close penetrates the exponentially smoothed moving average on the upside, a buy is placed on the opening tomorrow. If today's close penetrates the exponentially smoothed moving average on the downside, a sell is placed on the opening to-morrow.

3. The model is always in the market. When a new buy or sell signal is generated, the old position is liquidated simultaneously.

4. If the high and low of the next day are equal, then the assumption is made that the market is locked limit, and a trade cannot be made on that day. The trade will be done on the first day the market is not locked the limit.

Exponentially Smoothed Moving Average—
Results—Consistent Indicators

Table 3 gives the same type of analysis as was explained in the section on simple moving averages.

Linearly Weighted Moving Average
Constraints Defined

1. The linearly weighted moving average (L.W.M.A.) is calculated including today's close.

TABLE 3 EXPONENTIALLY SMOOTHED MOVING AVERAGES— TABLE OF RESULTS

	Best Day	(Best Range)	Cumulative Profits or Losses (Net)	Largest String of Losses	Number Trades	Number Profitable Trades	Number Losing Trades
Cocoa	57	52–61	$ 99,080	$−10,363	619	166	453
Corn	68	59–70	15,119	− 4,901	471	98	373
Sugar	69	68–70	172,985	−15,921	591	105	486
Cotton	70	60–70	35,855	−15,075	605	113	492
Silver	60	60–62	−61,400	−18,965	914	205	709
Copper	68	—	136,130	− 5,886	450	150	300
Soybeans	60	59–66	197,218	−13,600	708	142	566
Soybean Meal	62	—	8,486	−18,200	840	162	678
Wheat	70	66–70	13,570	−11,150	421	75	346
Pork Bellies	12	12–14	80,303	−11,177	1,217	401	816
Soybean Oil	66	65–69	82,904	− 6,730	677	160	517
Plywood	69	68–70	−24,526	− 5,002	467	104	363
Hogs	67	66–70	−11,834	−11,863	504	112	392

TABLE 4 LINEARLY WEIGHTED MOVING AVERAGES— TABLE OF RESULTS

	Best Day	(Best Range)	Cumulative Profits or Losses (Net)	Largest String of Losses	Number Trades	Number Profitable Trades	Number Losing Trades
Cocoa	52	51–55	$ 74,450	$− 8,773	796	206	590
Corn	65	63–70	21,779	− 5,487	524	118	406
Sugar	58	57–60	233,822	−14,063	707	149	558
Cotton	69	62–70	44,395	−18,070	731	139	592
Silver	45	45–51	−34,435	−20,920	1,036	297	739
Copper	68	67–70	124,848	−13,924	541	179	362
Soybeans	42	42–46	178,261	−19,100	892	213	697
Soybean Meal	41	37–43	31,385	−20,900	1,128	235	893
Wheat	70	65–70	52,495	− 9,000	403	94	309
Pork Bellies	28	25–36	81,625	− 9,222	815	267	548
Soybean Oil	34	29–41	106,996	− 5,470	1,198	303	895
Plywood	70	65–70	−22,273	− 5,138	470	109	361
Hogs	70	65–70	9,981	− 9,314	509	131	378

L.W.M.A. =

$$\frac{N \operatorname{Close}(M) + (N-1)\operatorname{Close}(M-1) + \cdots + (1)\operatorname{Close}(M-N+1)}{N + (N-1) + (N-2) + \cdots + 1}$$

where M = today's data (use only business days)
N = number of days

2. If today's close penetrates the linearly weighted moving average on the upside, a buy is placed on the opening tomorrow. If today's close penetrates the linearly weighted moving average on the downside, a sell is placed on the opening tomorrow.

3. The model is always in the market. When a new buy or sell signal is generated, the old position is liquidated simultaneously.

4. If the high and low of the next day are equal, then the assumption is made that the market is locked limit, and a trade cannot be made on that day. The trade will be done on the first day the market is not locked the limit.

Linearly Weighted Moving Average— Results—Consistent Indicators

Table 4 gives the same type of analysis as was explained in the section on simple moving averages.

Analysis of Results

We can now compare the three tables to arrive at the best of these strategies for each commodity. We will also examine some of the other interesting aspects that are revealed in this study.

Comparison

Table 5 gives the strategy that was consistent and showed the best cumulative net profits across the three types of averages.

Observations

1. Nine of the thirteen commodities analyzed show averages of 8 weeks or more to be the most consistent indicators of trend.

TABLE 5 CONSISTENT INDICATORS—
SIMPLE VS. EXPONENTIAL VS. LINEARLY
WEIGHTED MOVING AVERAGES

Cocoa	57-day	Exponentially smoothed
Corn	43-day	Simple
Sugar	60-day	Simple
Cotton	57-day	Simple
Silver	19-day	Simple
Copper	59-day	Simple
Soybeans	55-day	Simple
Soybean Meal	41-day	Linearly weighted
Wheat	41-day	Simple
Pork Bellies	19-day	Simple
Soybean Oil	34-day	Linearly weighted
Plywood	68-day	Simple
Hogs	16-day	Simple

TABLE 6

5 DAY

	Cumulative Profits or Losses (Net)	Largest String of Losses	Number of Trades	Number of Profitable Trades	Number of Losing Trades
SIMPLE MOVING AVERAGE					
Cocoa	$−356,193	$−39,202	2,934	767	2,167
Corn	−172,293	−12,323	2,171	501	1,670
Sugar	−294,127	−31,110	2,426	653	1,773
Cotton	−313,495	−46,045	2,483	698	1,785
Silver	−301,870	−23,700	3,633	971	2,662
Copper	−251,093	−20,196	3,067	994	2,073
Soybeans	−242,200	−46,175	2,918	870	2,048
Soybean Meal	−302,497	−29,800	3,235	783	2,452
Wheat	−236,252	−25,124	1,928	520	1,408
Pork Bellies	− 37,528	−18,378	2,066	670	1,396
Soybean Oil	−159,516	−13,824	3,342	945	2,397
Plywood	−221,041	−11,867	2,195	547	1,648
Hogs	−124,198	−12,293	2,657	746	1,911

46

TABLE 6 CONTINUED

5 DAY

	Cumulative Profits or Losses (Net)	Largest String of Losses	Number of Trades	Number of Profitable Trades	Number of Losing Trades
LINEARLY WEIGHTED MOVING AVERAGE					
Cocoa	$−475,834	$−40,762	3,478	899	2,597
Corn	−248,228	−20,781	2,472	554	1,918
Sugar	−398,281	−39,885	2,857	728	2,129
Cotton	−404,480	−37,630	2,919	791	2,128
Silver	−514,440	−31,600	4,419	1,155	3,264
Copper	−383,722	−26,020	3,682	1,112	2,570
Soybeans	−331,826	−34,775	3,395	989	2,406
Soybean Meal	−438,599	−36,190	3,844	931	2,913
Wheat	−349,043	−32,288	2,257	578	1,679
Pork Bellies	−142,841	−20,196	2,549	800	1,749
Soybean Oil	−262,976	−21,250	3,940	1,050	2,890
Plywood	−288,966	−17,048	2,633	618	2,015
Hogs	−172,662	−13,188	3,163	877	2,286
EXPONENTIALLY SMOOTHED MOVING AVERAGE					
Cocoa	$−368,450	$−42,432	2,945	711	2,234
Corn	−201,255	−16,125	2,530	498	2,032
Sugar	−334,415	−45,850	2,618	630	1,988
Cotton	−308,415	−31,190	2,533	681	1,852
Silver	−383,120	−33,175	3,763	942	2,821
Copper	−288,616	−20,996	3,044	921	2,123
Soybeans	−297,908	−44,575	3,235	863	2,372
Soybean Meal	−358,614	−38,980	3,324	760	2,564
Wheat	−258,163	−26,112	2,148	513	1,635
Pork Bellies	− 56,644	−14,723	2,064	602	1,462
Soybean Oil	−140,276	−14,524	3,475	915	2,560
Plywood	−222,398	−12,409	2,254	520	1,734
Hogs	−118,741	−13,389	2,696	734	1,962

TABLE 7

10 DAY

	Cumulative Profits or Losses (Net)	Largest String of Losses	Number of Trades	Number of Profitable Trades	Number of Losing Trades
SIMPLE MOVING AVERAGE					
Cocoa	$−202,645	$−29,095	1,864	487	1,377
Corn	−127,505	−13,996	1,530	335	1,195
Sugar	− 88,293	−34,024	1,654	393	1,261
Cotton	−166,870	−29,285	1,743	439	1,304
Silver	−118,270	−20,935	2,309	613	1,696
Copper	−154,570	−19,374	1,880	591	1,228
Soybeans	+ 27,247	−40,250	1,831	532	1,299
Soybean Meal	−214,070	−31,410	2,214	505	1,709
Wheat	−147,851	−18,900	1,260	319	941
Pork Bellies	+ 22,239	−10,338	1,394	446	948
Soybean Oil	− 23,668	−11,050	2,189	590	1,599
Plywood	−122,229	− 9,036	1,412	350	1,062
Hogs	− 21,681	− 9,494	1,632	487	1,145
LINEARLY WEIGHTED MOVING AVERAGE					
Cocoa	$−275,166	$−33,493	2,301	562	1,739
Corn	−152,026	−13,110	1,840	390	1,450
Sugar	−191,362	−40,500	2,045	484	1,561
Cotton	−211,720	−19,035	2,042	562	1,480
Silver	−227,690	−25,975	2,852	760	2,092
Copper	−180,916	−19,972	2,315	695	1,620
Soybeans	− 53,718	−47,075	2,390	697	1,693
Soybean Meal	−243,244	−35,390	2,679	609	2,070
Wheat	−172,995	−20,712	1,501	397	1,104
Pork Bellies	+ 5,171	−13,828	1,667	524	1,143
Soybean Oil	− 46,412	−10,460	2,710	731	1,979
Plywood	−160,086	− 9,397	1,812	451	1,361
Hogs	− 61,172	− 9,470	2,121	610	1,511

TABLE 7 CONTINUED

10 DAY

	Cumulative Profits or Losses (Net)	Largest String of Losses	Number of Trades	Number of Profitable Trades	Number of Losing Trades
EXPONENTIALLY SMOOTHED MOVING AVERAGE					
Cocoa	$−172,684	$−25,863	2,086	522	1,564
Corn	−139,413	−14,310	1,749	348	1,401
Sugar	−124,172	−30,008	1,854	403	1,451
Cotton	−124,835	−34,175	1,788	458	1,330
Silver	−210,370	−32,810	2,615	655	1,960
Copper	−122,322	−16,073	1,971	611	1,360
Soybeans	− 25,580	−36,250	2,170	563	1,607
Soybean Meal	−219,037	−37,390	2,382	531	1,851
Wheat	−144,751	−18,800	1,486	340	1,146
Pork Bellies	+ 57,393	−12,943	1,386	449	937
Soybean Oil	− 31,358	−12,638	2,356	602	1,754
Plywood	−135,622	− 9,340	1,556	357	1,199
Hogs	− 35,725	−12,898	1,743	476	1,267

TABLE 8

20 DAY

	Cumulative Profits or Losses (Net)	Largest String of Losses	Number of Trades	Number of Profitable Trades	Number of Losing Trades
SIMPLE MOVING AVERAGE					
Cocoa	$+ 15,681	$−14,940	1,215	351	864
Corn	− 50,223	− 6,837	980	205	775
Sugar	+ 96,618	−16,713	1,143	263	880
Cotton	− 73,945	−19,640	1,159	271	888
Silver	+ 29,125	−22,375	1,267	404	863
Copper	+ 21,284	−12,810	1,209	382	817
Soybeans	+154,315	−19,550	1,182	322	860
Soybean Meal	+ 90	−32,100	1,414	295	1,119
Wheat	− 55,172	-17,300	794	188	606
Pork Bellies	+ 84,832	− 9,476	758	266	492
Soybean Oil	+ 78,810	− 8,414	1,290	332	958
Plywood	− 86,297	−11,454	928	210	718
Hogs	+ 26,522	− 8,147	1,020	268	734

TABLE 8 CONTINUED

20 DAY

	Cumulative Profits or Losses (Net)	Largest String of Losses	Number of Trades	Number of Profitable Trades	Number of Losing Trades
LINEARLY WEIGHTED MOVING AVERAGE					
Cocoa	$− 52,413	$−18,250	1,578	399	1,179
Corn	− 72,921	−10,274	1,198	260	938
Sugar	+ 35,375	−19,152	1,359	304	1,055
Cotton	− 99,795	−25,700	1,430	343	1,087
Silver	−180,680	−32,745	2,009	519	1,490
Copper	− 55,420	−12,135	1,557	499	1,058
Soybeans	+ 72,682	−29,150	1,581	432	1,149
Soybean Meal	−140,704	−33,130	1,858	390	1,468
Wheat	− 69,666	−18,150	1,063	263	800
Pork Bellies	+ 79,203	− 9,050	1,006	327	679
Soybean Oil	+ 3,050	−12,820	1,796	481	1,315
Plywood	−120,779	−11,225	1,228	288	940
Hogs	+ 8,705	− 9,565	1,299	363	936
EXPONENTIALLY SMOOTHED MOVING AVERAGE					
Cocoa	$+ 6,691	$−15,385	1,295	350	945
Corn	− 58,777	−10,698	1,170	232	938
Sugar	+ 79,154	−16,745	1,299	268	1,031
Cotton	− 60,965	−20,825	1,229	279	950
Silver	−129,045	−27,885	1,752	437	1,315
Copper	+ 26,912	−13,546	1,274	408	866
Soybeans	+100,753	−17,850	1,477	373	1,104
Soybean Meal	− 52,193	−28,900	1,568	329	1,239
Wheat	− 45,558	−19,900	946	209	737
Pork Bellies	+ 51,444	−11,966	911	269	642
Soybean Oil	+ 73,124	− 8,910	1,595	411	1,184
Plywood	− 91,373	− 9,898	1,080	240	840
Hogs	− 13,704	−11,215	1,181	303	878

2. The ratio of profitable trades to total trades usually ranges between 1:3 and 1:4 for most of the consistent indicators.

3. The largest string of losses at any point in time has ranged from about $6000 to $21,000 per commodity. It is unlikely that all commodities would be down their maximum at the same time, but that remote probability does exist. These numbers do not include initial margin.

4. The cumulative net profits over the period analyzed for the consistent indicators looks good for all except plywood, which has not performed well under any of these three strategies.

5. Consistent moving averages tended to cluster near the most consistent one.

Conclusion

Most of the commodities tested showed that they worked best with longer-term trend indicators. We can also see that in most cases the simple moving average works better than either the linear or the exponential average. This should put to rest some of the criticism leveled against the simple moving average.

It can also be seen that our consistent indicators worked much more efficiently than either the 5-, 10-, or 20-day averages. As explained earlier, our indicators were the most consistent for the number of days ranging from 3 to 70 days.

A trader using these averages must be disciplined enough to take the signals and wait for the next signal, and should have enough risk capital to absorb sizable losses. Of course, one way to minimize risk is to diversify a portfolio. Also, the ratio of profitable to total trades is usually 25 to 35%, so a speculator must be able psychologically to cope with a series of losses in order to take advantage of possible profits. In summary, a mechanical approach needs a well-disciplined trader.

CHANNELS AND CROSSOVERS

An Explanation and Computerized Testing of Commodity Trading Techniques

FRANK HOCHHEIMER

This is the second in a series of research reports that examine major technical strategies used by commodity speculators. The first article, entitled "Moving Averages, An Explanation and Computerized Testing of Simple, Linear, and Exponentially Smoothed Moving Averages" dated February 1978 (pages 39–51) can be used as background reference. The highlights of this previous research report are reviewed for comparison with the four additional strategies tested and examined in this report. For consistency, the period analyzed is from January 1970 through December 1976, for every contract for each of the commodities given in Table 1.

It was assumed that each contract was traded from its inception to the last business day prior to expiration month.

Reprinted by permission of Merrill, Lynch, Pierce Fenner & Smith.

TABLE 1   COMMODITIES ANALYZED

Copper	Cocoa	Soybean Meal
Silver	Corn	Soybean Oil
Cotton	Wheat	Pork Bellies
Sugar	Soybeans	Hogs
	Plywood	Cattle

Methodology

A weighting method was constructed to weight the results of each contract as to cumulative profits, largest string of losses, and the ratio of profits to losses.   This method was applied to each contract simulated for each model and for each strategy.   By a series of sorting procedures, a consistent approach to the market was sought.   Our search was not for the optimal strategy in each contract individually but for a strategy that would consistently perform well according to our weighting system over time in the model.   The same weighting method was used in the previous moving average study.   A word of caution is in order here. As with all historical testing procedures, success in the past is in no way a guarantee of success in the future.   The results are offered as a guide to those speculators and hedgers who use these systems.

We are not only interested in arriving at a consistent indicator for the above commodities using various strategies within a model, but we are also interested in comparing models and indicating which model and strategy works best, that is, comparing the consistent strategies for the hog market using moving averages, exponential smoothing, crossovers, and the like.   To this end we will be examining four additional models in this article and testing them using various strategies.

Concepts Explained

The first model tested is the crossover of two simple moving averages. The two averages consist of a short-term and a longer-term average.   The short average varied from 3 to 25 days, and the longer average varied from 5 to 50 days.   Every combination for every contract in our time period was tested and weighted.   The crossover method is one way in which the whipsaw effect seen in simple moving averages can be minimized.

Another approach is the channel approach and is a complete departure from the moving average systems. In the channel studies, a certain number of days back are examined for high and low values, a penetration of these values signals a trade. There are many variations of these channel models, and we have tested three for this article. The channels range from 3 to 70 days back in time. We are seeking to find an approach to each market that has been shown to work consistently well in the past. The results shown in Figure 1 are for informational purposes only. They are computer simulations using assumptions that most closely fit actual market trading conditions.

Crossover of Two Simple Moving Averages Constraints Defined

1. The average of M days' closes and N days' closes are calculated where $M < N$ (M is less than N).

   The averages include today's close and use only business days.

2. If average $M >$ average N (average M greater than average N), a buy is placed on the opening tomorrow. If average M < average N (average M is less than average N), a sell is placed on the opening tomorrow.

3. The model is always in the market. When a new buy or sell signal is generated, the old position is liquidated simultaneously.

4. If the high and low of the next day are equal, then the assumption is made that the market is locked limit, and a trade cannot be made on that day. The trade will be done on the first day the market is not locked the limit.

If the short-term average is above the long-term average, one should be long, and if the short-term average is below the long-term average, one should be short. Figure 1 is an example of this type of model.

Crossovers of Two Simple Moving Averages Results—Consistent Indicators

Table 2 gives the most consistent crossovers in column 1. Column 2 shows cumulative net profit for all contracts traded in the 1970–1976 period (defined previously) using current Merrill Lynch commissions

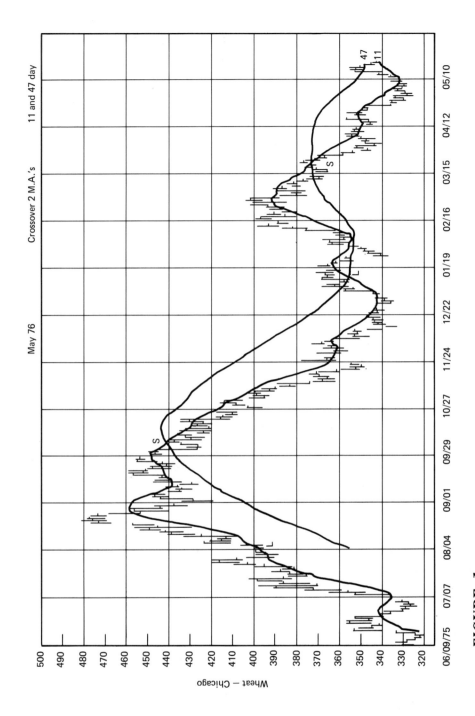

FIGURE 1
Crossover, 2 M.A.'s—11 and 47 day; May 1976 wheat.

56

**TABLE 2   CROSSOVERS OF TWO SIMPLE AVERAGES—
TABLE OF RESULTS**

	Best Day	*Cumulative Profits or Losses (Net)*	*Largest String of Losses*	*Number Trades*	*Number Profitable Trades*	*Number Losing Trades*
Cocoa	7,25	$176,940	$− 4,436	468	199	269
Corn	11,47	69,275	− 2,697	225	93	132
Sugar	5,50	335,843	−13,851	311	109	202
Cotton	16,25	304,485	− 4,755	485	233	252
Silver	3,26	100,790	− 8,610	661	262	399
Copper	17,33	212,939	− 3,057	354	177	177
Soybeans	16,50	286,440	−15,665	311	148	163
Soybean Meal	18,50	117,155	− 8,155	272	118	154
Wheat	11,47	133,118	− 2,660	209	87	122
Pork Bellies	25,46	13,124	−21,538	226	100	126
Soybean Oil	14,50	121,749	− 6,585	327	128	199
Plywood	24,42	18,505	− 3,184	219	100	119
Hogs	3,14	97,448	− 7,805	793	321	472
Cattle	7,13	147,540	− 4,605	792	337	455

---

and current contract point values.   Column 3 indicates the largest string of losses in any one contract not including margin money.   Columns 4, 5, and 6 show total number of trades, total number of profitable trades, and total number of losing trades, respectively, for all contracts traded in the test period.

Intraday Closing Price Channel Constraints Defined

1. The highest and lowest closing price of the last N days are found.

2. A buy signal is generated if the price on day $(N + 1)$ exceeds the highest close of the last N days.   A sell signal is generated if the price on day $(N + 1)$ is lower than the lowest close of the last N days.   Stop orders are used to initiate action on penetration.   Only one position can be signaled per day.

3. The model is always in the market.   When a new buy or sell signal is generated, the old position is liquidated simultaneously.

4. If the high and low of the day are equal, then the assumption is made that the market is locked limit, and a trade cannot be made on that day. The trade will be done on the opening the first day the market is not locked the limit.

If you count back the proper number of days and find the highest and lowest close in that period, you have a channel. If today's action is above the upper value, liquidate short and go long or stay long. If today's action is below the lower value, liquidate long and go short or stay short. If action is within channel, maintain position. It is possible for both parts of the channel to be penetrated in one day. Only the first signal is taken.

Intraday Closing Price Channel Results— Consistent Indicators

Table 3 gives the same type of analysis as was explained in the section on crossovers of simple moving averages.

TABLE 3 INTRADAY CLOSING PRICE CHANNEL— TABLE OF RESULTS

	Best Day	Cumulative Profits or Losses (Net)	Largest String of Losses	Number Trades	Number Profitable Trades	Number Losing Trades
Cocoa	53	$135,689	$− 7,460	118	65	53
Corn	38	40,834	− 5,798	159	66	93
Sugar	50	281,629	−16,687	119	54	65
Cotton	61	162,520	−12,685	110	48	62
Silver	15	87,470	−13,060	603	282	321
Copper	32	178,774	− 5,800	204	113	91
Soybeans	49	256,856	−10,525	157	76	81
Soybean Meal	57	79,818	−12,602	311	66	245
Wheat	30	118,503	− 4,580	173	82	91
Pork Bellies	5	196,521	−10,370	1,414	567	847
Soybean Oil	47	135,804	− 9,086	162	76	86
Plywood	49	8,632	− 4,432	120	57	63
Hogs	10	87,061	− 8,425	743	299	444
Cattle	13	96,500	−10,990	572	229	343

Interday Closing Price Channels Constraints Defined

1. The highest and lowest closing price of the last N days are found.

2. A buy signal is generated if the close on day $(N + 1)$ exceeds the highest close of the last N days. A sell signal is generated if the price on day $(N + 1)$ is lower than the lowest close of the last N days. Trades will be made on the next day's opening.

3. The model is always in the market. When a new buy or sell signal is generated, the old position is liquidated simultaneously.

4. If the high and low of the next day are equal, then the assumption is made that the market is locked limit, and a trade cannot be made on that day. The trade will be done on the first day the market is not locked the limit.

If you count back the proper number of days and find the highest and lowest close in the period you have a channel. If today's close is above the upper value, liquidate short and go long or stay long. If today's close is below the lower value, liquidate long and go short or stay short. If close is within channel, maintain position. Figure 2 shows places where such a model would have taken positions.

Interday Closing Price Channel Results— Consistent Indicators

Table 4 gives the same type of analysis as was explained in the section on crossovers of simple moving averages.

Intraday Extreme Price Channel Constraints Defined

1. The highest high and the lowest low on the last N days are found.

2. A buy signal is generated if the price on day $(N + 1)$ exceeds the highest high of the last N days. A sell signal is generated if the price on day $(N + 1)$ is lower than the lowest low of the last N days. Stop orders are used to initiate action on penetration. Only one position can be signaled per day.

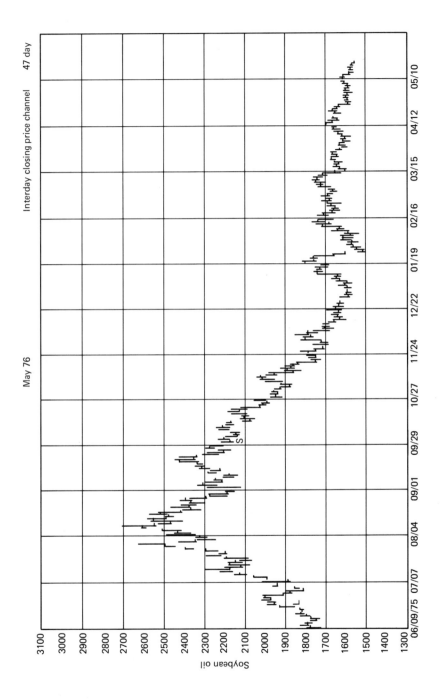

FIGURE 2
Interday closing price channel—47 day; May 1976 soybean oil.

TABLE 4 INTERDAY CLOSING PRICE CHANNEL— TABLE OF RESULTS

	Best Day	Cumulative Profits or Losses (Net)	Largest String of Losses	Number Trades	Number Profitable Trades	Number Losing Trades
Cocoa	53	$147,913	$− 6,248	110	60	50
Corn	49	39,533	− 5,048	118	50	68
Sugar	40	296,027	−20,758	133	57	76
Cotton	62	206,575	− 6,870	89	48	41
Silver	14	27,690	−12,365	552	212	340
Copper	27	151,671	− 7,225	217	115	102
Soybeans	51	244,839	−11,325	120	68	52
Soybean Meal	49	104,690	− 7,000	166	71	95
Wheat	23	111,087	− 6,900	205	80	125
Pork Bellies	52	60,263	− 9,892	94	51	43
Soybean Oil	41	157,540	− 5,740	157	82	75
Plywood	51	8,646	− 3,622	109	48	61
Hogs	9	83,702	− 9,854	606	253	353
Cattle	9	95,480	− 4,790	577	223	354

3. The model is always in the market. When a new buy or sell signal is generated, the old position is liquidated simultaneously.

4. If the high and low of the next day are equal, then the assumption is made that the market is locked limit, and a trade cannot be made on that day. The trade will be done on the opening the first day the market is not locked the limit.

This model operates under the same assumptions as the intraday closing price channel, except that the high value of the channel is the highest high, and the low value of the channel is the lowest low of the last N days.

Intraday Extreme Price Channel Results— Consistent Indicators

Table 5 gives the same type of analysis as was explained in the section on crossovers of simple moving averages.

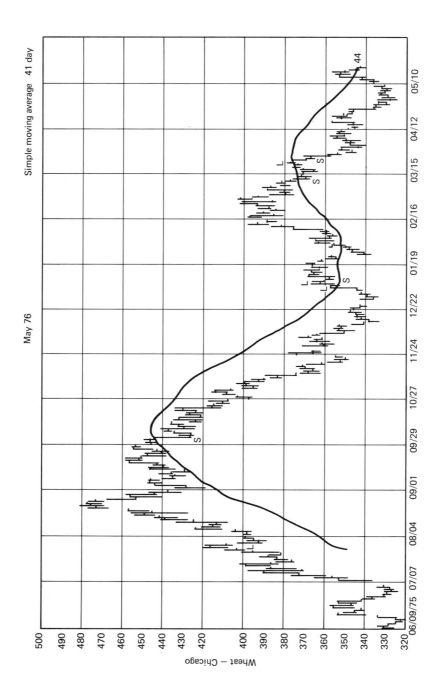

FIGURE 3
Simple moving average—41 day; May 1976 wheat.

62

TABLE 5   INTRADAY EXTREME PRICE CHANNEL—
TABLE OF RESULTS

	Best Day	Cumulative Profits or Losses (Net)	Largest String of Losses	Number Trades	Number Profitable Trades	Number Losing Trades
Cocoa	18	$144,912	$− 7,350	357	156	201
Corn	38	45,812	− 5,599	138	59	79
Sugar	40	284,745	−23,647	134	61	73
Cotton	70	152,530	−14,510	90	43	47
Silver	4	147,095	− 8,375	1,866	718	1,148
Copper	29	163,013	−10,675	208	112	96
Soybeans	51	213,904	−10,925	130	68	62
Soybean Meal	57	71,603	−12,792	148	66	82
Wheat	22	113,239	− 7,500	219	86	133
Pork Bellies	38	89,274	− 7,750	129	63	66
Soybean Oil	42	145,002	− 5,740	156	80	76
Plywood	48	7,789	− 3,622	115	53	62
Hogs	8	53,440	− 8,480	720	284	436
Cattle	13	93,450	−11,150	433	184	249

Summary of Consistent Indicators Found in the Moving Average Study

A synopsis of the consistent indicators found in the study on moving averages follows. The most consistent averages with the best number and results are presented in Table 6. We then have a basis for comparison with the models tested in this article. See Figure 3 for samples of trades under the simple moving average model.

Analysis of Results

We can now compare the results of the seven different models tested so far to arrive at the best of these strategies for each commodity. Further observations will also be made as to some of the conclusions that can be drawn from the data.

TABLE 6 SYNOPSIS OF MOVING AVERAGES—TABLE OF RESULTS

	Best Day	Aver-age Type	Cumula-tive Profits or Losses (Net)	Largest String of Losses	Number Trades	Number Profit-able Trades	Number Losing Trades
Cocoa	57	2	$ 99,080	$−10,363	619	166	453
Corn	43	1	24,646	− 6,537	565	126	439
Sugar	60	1	270,402	−15,563	492	99	393
Cotton	57	1	68,685	−11,330	641	121	520
Silver	19	1	42,920	−15,285	1,393	429	964
Copper	59	1	165,143	− 7,687	432	158	274
Soybeans	55	1	222,195	−10,800	728	151	577
Soybean Meal	41	3	31,385	−20,900	1,128	235	893
Wheat	41	1	65,806	−12,550	480	124	356
Pork Bellies	19	1	97,925	− 9,498	774	281	493
Soybean Oil	34	3	106,996	− 5,470	1,198	303	895
Plywood	68	1	1,622	− 3,929	372	98	274
Hogs	16	1	35,595	− 7,190	1,093	318	775
Cattle	40	3	32,420	− 6,930	830	210	620

Type Average: 1—Simple Moving Average 2—Exponentially Smoothed
3—Linearly Weighted

TABLE 7 CONSISTENT INDICATORS—SIMPLE VS. EXPONENTIAL VS. LINEAR VS. CROSSOVERS VS. INTRADAY CLOSING PRICE CHANNEL VS. INTERDAY CLOSING PRICE CHANNEL VS. INTRADAY EXTREME PRICE CHANNELS

Commodity	Strategy	Model
Cocoa	7 and 25	Crossover
Corn	11 and 47	Crossover
Sugar	5 and 50	Crossover
Cotton	16 and 25	Crossover
Silver	4	Intraday extreme price channel
Copper	17 and 33	Crossover
Soybeans	16 and 50	Crossover
Soybean Meal	18 and 50	Crossover
Wheat	11 and 47	Crossover
Pork Bellies	5	Intraday closing price channel
Soybean Oil	41	Interday closing price channel
Plywood	24 and 42	Crossover
Hogs	3 and 14	Crossover
Cattle	7 and 13	Crossover

Table 7 above gives the strategy and model which was consistent and showed the best cumulative net profits across the seven types of models tested.

Observations

1. Eleven of the fourteen commodities showed crossovers to be the most consistent model.

2. The ratio of profits to losses is usually better than 1:2.

3. The largest strings of losses range from $2660 to $21,660, but more than 50% are below $5000.

4. Cumulative net profits for all contracts between 1970 through 1976 are all above $69,000, except for plywood, which although performance has improved, still lags far behind the other commodities tested.

Conclusions

All the commodities tested showed that improvement could be achieved over a straightforward moving average model, even when linear weighting or exponential smoothing are added. With crossovers, as well as channels, the whipsaw effect so often seen in simple moving averages can be reduced. It should be noted that a trader using these models must be disciplined enough to take the signals and wait for the next signal, and should have enough risk capital to absorb sizable losses. Of course, one way to minimize risk is to diversify a portfolio. Also, the ratio of profitable to total trades is usually less than 50%, so a speculator must be able psychologically to cope with a series of losses in order to take advantage of possible profits. In summary, a mechanical approach needs a well-disciplined trader.

J. Welles Wilder approached the commodity markets by a relatively circuitous route. It included a degree in mechanical engineering, a stint designing machines to automate clothing manufacture, and far-flung and very successful real estate development enterprises in North Carolina and Virginia.

It was just about the time the commodity markets captured his imagination that his payoff from his real estate ventures made it possible for him to devote full time to commodity research. In 1972 he bought a computer, opened a small office, and began.

In 1974 he founded Trend Research, a company devoted exclusively to commodity market analysis. His recent excellent book, New Concepts in Technical Trading Systems, *presents his original work. The following treatise is drawn largely from that book.*

There are three critical areas of analysis for the speculator: the selection of a system for entering and exiting the market; the allocation of resources to the entire combined speculative effort and its distribution within a "portfolio"; and the selection of which items to trade. Most research effort has been in the area of systems analysis and development, and least in the selection process.

The selection process is equally as important as determining your entry and exit timing. If you choose a commodity that does not conform to the characteristics of your system, it will most often lose money for you, instead of earning profits. Since most systems are trend following in nature, it is beneficial to spend additional time to determine which commodities are trending before following the system's buy-and-sell signals.

Consider the advantage of reducing the number of commodities in a diversified portfolio from 20 items of uncertain traits to five with high-performance profiles. The extreme diversification of the large portfolio, necessary because it is uncertain which of the commodities in the large group will be the high-performance elements, generally works to reduce opportunity more than it helps to reduce risk. A selection process that identifies the potentially better performers can offer reasonable diversification with considerably more opportunity—a better risk/reward ratio. Without a selection process, the largest part of the portfolio will constantly serve to offset the profits of the few successful elements.

J. Welles Wilder, Jr. presents new insight into selection of high-potential commodities in his article "Selection and Direction." He establishes a new index *that is based on the four essential components of price movement and investment: the trending factor, the volatility of prices, the margin, and brokerage commissions. It is both unique and sensible, presented in a clear manner using examples, and allows each investor to test the method himself.*

The commodity selection index *presented here represents a major effort by Wilder, and we are pleased to include it. For those readers interested in pursuing his approach, further information can be received by contacting J. Welles Wilder, Jr., Trend Research, P.O. Box 450, Greensboro, North Carolina, 27402. A more comprehensive discussion of the material is published in Wilder's book,* New Concepts in Technical Analysis, *available through Trend Research.*

SELECTION AND DIRECTION

J. WELLES WILDER, Jr.

Most mechanical trading systems are trend-following systems. All trend-following systems have one thing in common; that is, they are usually very profitable when the market is in a good trending mode and usually unprofitable in a nontrending, sideways market.

If you use a trend-following mechanical method, consider the advantage of having an index that would continuously rate a commodity as to how much it is trending. If this rating scale is within constant perimeters, say, between 0 and 100, then all commodities could be compared to each other on the same basis. Imagine having available to you each week a listing of all commodities arranged in order of which are trending the most.

Going a few steps further would make the index even better. A commodity can be in a good trending mode (highly directional) but moving very slowly. Another commodity can also be in a good trending mode but moving very fast. Let's then make this index also be a function of volatility to show a higher index value for a commodity that is not only in a good trending mode but also moving faster.

While we're at it, let's consider two other factors: margin requirement and commission costs. For instance, coffee may be the highest commodity on the index scale, but if the margin requirement is $15,000 per contract, then we might be better off to trade five contracts of soybeans with a $3000 margin requirement per contract than to trade the one contract of coffee.

The commission cost is probably the least significant consideration, so we will give it a very small weighting in the index.

Now our index not only tells us which commodities are trending the most but also considers how fast a commodity is moving in the trend, and it tells us how good a deal the commodity is relative to margin requirement and commission cost.

At this point, you are probably thinking that this all sounds good, but can such an index really be defined? Here is my approach to developing this index. I call this the *commodity selection index*. The first problem is to define a trend. Simply stated, a trend is directional movement as opposed to nondirectional or random movement. For the purpose of this discussion, let's define a trend in terms of the concept of directional movement. To do this, we start with the smallest increment of directional movement. In Figure 1, movement is obviously in the up direction. The magnitude of this up movement is the difference between points *C* and *A*. In effect, this is the high today minus the high yesterday. We will call this distance *plus DM* (+*DM*). Because the movement is up, we consider only the highs. We disregard the distance between the lows, that is, points *B* and *D*. In Figure 2, the directional movement is obviously down. The directional distance is the difference between points *B* and *D*. This distance is considered to be a minus distance and is the difference between the low today and the low yesterday.

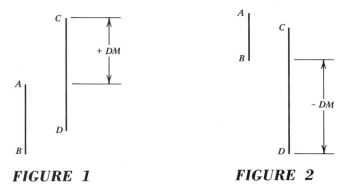

FIGURE 1   **FIGURE 2**

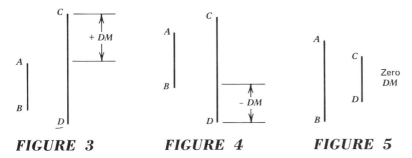

FIGURE 3   FIGURE 4   FIGURE 5

Since the direction is obviously down, we are concerned only with the lows. We disregard the distance between the highs. I will call the difference between the lows *minus DM* ($-DM$).

Now, how do we handle an outside day? Look at Figure 3. In this case the directional movement is up because $+DM$ is greater than $-DM$. *Directional movement must be either up or down—it cannot be a combination of both.* We therefore consider the larger *DM* for an outside day and disregard the smaller *DM*. Here, the *DM*, which is the distance between C and A, is plus.

In Figure 4, only $-DM$ is considered because it is larger than $+DM$.

How about an inside day (Figure 5)? In this case directional movement is zero. In Figure 6, the directional movement is also zero.

On a limit up day (Figure 7), the $+DM$ is C minus A. On a limit down day (Figure 8), the $-DM$ is B minus D. These illustrations take into consideration every possible configuration that could occur between two days relative to directional movement. To sum the preceding in one sentence, we could define:

> **The basic increment of directional movement**—*the largest part of today's range that is outside yesterday's range.*

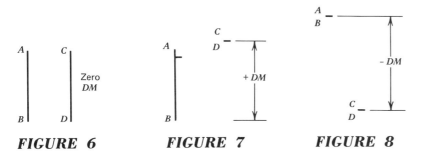

FIGURE 6   FIGURE 7   FIGURE 8

If the largest part of today's range is *above* yesterday's range, the *DM* is *plus*. If the largest part of today's range is *below* yesterday's range, the *DM* is *minus*.

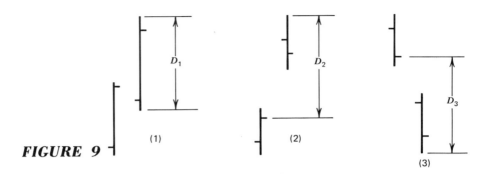

FIGURE 9

To be meaningful, *DM* must be expressed as a function of range; that is, it must be relative to range. The range increment is today's true range (TR_1). This is the *largest* of the following (Figure 9):

1. The distance between today's high and today's low (D_1).

2. The distance between today's high and yesterday's close. (D_2).

3. The distance between today's low and yesterday's close (D_3).

True range is always considered to be a positive number.

To make directional movement relative to range, we simply divide directional movement by the true range. This gives us what we call the *directional indicator* (*DI*). The $+DI$ and $-DI$ equations below each express the *directional indicator* for *one day* which is indicated by the subscript $(_1)$.

$$+DI_1 = \frac{+DM_1}{TR_1}$$

$$-DI_1 = \frac{-DM_1}{TR_1}$$

If the day were an *up* day, the $+DI_1$ equation would be applicable; if the day were a *down* day, the $-DI_1$ equation would be applicable. We cannot have both directional movement up and directional movement down on the same day. Today is either *up* or it is *down*. In effect, the $+DI$ is an expression of the percent of the true range that is *up* for the day; the $-DI$ is an expression of the percent of the true range that is *down* for the day.

To make the directional indicator a usable tool, we must obtain the sum of the *DIs* for a period of time. We use 14 days because that is an average half-cycle period. This can be done by reviewing the preceding 14 days and determining the directional movement (DM_i) for each day. We also determine the *true range* (TR_i) for each day. First, we add together all of the true ranges for the 14 days. We designate the sum of the 14 days' ranges as TR_{14}. Next, we add together all the plus *DMs* ($+DM_i$) for the 14 days and call the sum $+DM_{14}$. Now we go back and add all the minus *DMs* ($-DM_i$) for the 14 days and call the sum $-DM_{14}$.

The equations for $+DI_{14}$ and $-DI_{14}$ are as follows:

$$+DI_{14} = \frac{+DM_{14}}{TR_{14}}$$

$$-DI_{14} = \frac{-DM_{14}}{TR_{14}}$$

(The definition "minus *DM*" is a description of downward movement; it is *not* treated as a minus number in the equation.)

Once we have determined the first $+DI_{14}$ and the first $-DI_{14}$, it is no longer necessary to keep up with 14 days' back data to determine the $+DI_{14}$ and $-DI_{14}$ for the following day. We use the previous day's data and an accumulation technique in this determination. The advantage to using the accumulation technique is:

1. It eliminates the necessity of keeping up with 14 days' previous data.

2. It incorporates a smoothing effect on the *DMs*.

To obtain the new $+DM_{14}$ using the accumulation technique, take yesterday's $+DM_{14}$, divide it by 14, and subtract this amount from yesterday's $+DM_{14}$. Next, add back the $+DM_1$ for today, if any. The result is the $+DM_{14}$ for today.

$$\text{today's } +DM_{14} = \text{previous } +DM_{14} - \left[\frac{\text{previous } +DM_{14}}{14} \right] + \text{today's } +DM_1$$

We do the same thing with the $-DM_{14}$. We subtract $1/14$th of yesterday's $-DM_{14}$ and add back the $-DM_1$ today, if any.

$$\text{today's } -DM_{14} = \text{previous } -DM_{14} - \left[\frac{\text{previous } -DM_{14}}{14} \right] + \text{today's } -DM_1$$

Each day we will be taking away $1/14$th of the $+DM$ and $1/14$th of the $-DM$. If the DM_1 (today) is minus, we will add its value back to the $-DM_{14}$. If the DM_1 (today) is plus, we will add it back to the $+DM_{14}$.

The same procedure is used on the true range. We reduce TR_{14} by $1/14$th and add back to it the true range for today (TR_1). The result is our new TR_{14}.

$$\text{today's } TR_{14} = \text{previous } TR_{14} - \left[\frac{\text{previous } TR_{14}}{14} \right] + \text{today's } TR_1$$

The following equations are not in the book *New Concepts in Technical Trading Systems;* however, they are easier to use and produce the same results.

$$\text{today's } +DM_{14} = .93 \text{ (previous } +DM_{14}) + \text{today's } +DM_1$$
$$\text{today's } -DM_{14} = .93 \text{ (previous } -DM_{14}) + \text{today's } -DM_1$$
$$\text{today's } \quad TR_{14} = .93 \text{ (previous } \quad TR_{14}) + \text{today's } TR_1$$

$$+DI_{14} = \frac{+DM_{14}}{TR_{14}} \qquad\qquad -DI_{14} = \frac{-DM_{14}}{TR_{14}}$$

The $+DI_{14}$ is an indication of the percent of the *total* true range of the last 14 days that was *up*. The $-DI_{14}$ is an indication of the percent of the *total* true range of the last 14 days that was *down*. Both the $+DI$ and the $-DI$ are positive numbers. Suppose that:

$$+DM_{14} = \quad 8.82$$
$$-DM_{14} = 15.75$$
$$TR_{14} = 43.32$$

This means that for the last 14 days the up directional movement is 8.82, the down directional movement is 15.75, and the total movement is 43.32.

$$+DI_{14} = \frac{8.82}{43.32} = .20$$

$$-DI_{14} = \frac{15.75}{43.32} = .36$$

therefore, 20% of the directional movement was up and 36% of the directional movement was down.

Now let's analyze what we have here. If 20% of the true range for the past 14 days was up and 36% of the true range for the past 14 days was down, then we add these two figures together and determine that 56% of the true range was directional—either up or down; therefore, 44% of the true range was nondirectional.

The important concept here is that:

> **True directional movement** is the difference between $+DI_{14}$ and $-DI_{14}$.

This is a significant concept. *The more directional the movement of a commodity or stock, the greater will be the difference between $+DI_{14}$ and $-DI_{14}$.* Each day we have a plus-directional movement, we are *adding* to $+DI_{14}$. At the same time we are *subtracting* from $-DI_{14}$. If the direction were up for 14 or more consecutive days, the $+DI_{14}$ would have a large value, and the $-DI_{14}$ would approach zero. Therefore, the difference between the two would be very large.

Conversely, if the price were to go down for 14 or more consecutive days, giving us a $-DM$ for every day, we would be *adding* to the $-DI_{14}$ and *subtracting* from the $+DI_{14}$, thereby increasing the difference between $+DI_{14}$ and $-DI_{14}$.

If the price were meandering in a sideways direction, then the difference between $+DI_{14}$ and $-DI_{14}$ would be very small. This tells us the price is moving *nondirectionally*. Notice also that we can have a high directional movement value in a very slow-moving market, because directional movement is a function of daily range. Conversely, we can have a low directional movement value in a very volatile market.

Now let's take the difference between the $+DI_{14}$ and the $-DI_{14}$ which represents directional movement and divide this by the sum of the two.

We call the difference taken in this way DX.

$$DX = \frac{DI \ difference}{DI \ sum}$$

Using the numbers in the previous example:

$$DX = \frac{15.75 - 8.82}{15.75 + 8.82} = .29$$

Dropping the decimal point gives you a value for DX of 29. The equation results in a DX that must always be between 0 and 100. The higher the DX, the more directional the movement. The lower the DX, the less directional the movement.

Suppose that the price goes straight up for 14 days or more and then turns around and goes straight down for 14 days or more. The DX will decrease as the price tops out and starts down, and it will increase again as the price continues down. Both the *up move* and the *down move* represent good directional movement. As the price tops out and starts down, the *difference* between the $+DI_{14}$ and the $-DI_{14}$ *will decrease, go to zero, and then increase.* That is, as the price is going up, $+DI_{14}$ will be a large number and $-DI_{14}$ will be a smaller number. As the price tops out and goes down, *the equilibrium point will be reached,* then the $-DI_{14}$ will increase and the $+DI_{41}$ will decrease, and therefore the *difference* will again increase.

To smooth out this action relative to DX and make DX indicative of both extreme *up* and *down* price movement, the period for determining DX must be twice the period for determining $+DI_{14}$ and $-DI_{14}$. This can be accomplished simply by using a 14-day average of DX. We compute the DX for 14 days and then at that time begin determining the *average directional movement index (ADX)* from the previous day's *ADX.*

The equation for the ADX also uses only yesterday's data. The ADX equation presented here is a little simpler than the equation in the book *New Concepts in Technical Trading Systems* and can be immediately recognized as the exponential moving average equation:

$$ADX_{today} = ADX_{previous} + .07 \ (ADX_{previous} - DX_{today})$$

Since the ADX is a function of the DX, it will have excessive variance at tops and bottoms. To compensate for the variance, we use a 14-day differential of the ADX as the final rating factor for directional movement. We call this final rating factor the average directional movement index rating ($ADXR$):

$$ADXR = \left[\frac{ADX_{\text{today}} + ADX_{14 \text{ days ago}}}{2} \right]$$

Since the $ADXR$ is used only as a rating of directional movement, it must be indicative of directional movement; at the same time it must have a minimum fluctuation when directional movement changes direction.

The ADX, when plotted, tends to form a sine curve on the $ADXR$ scale (Figure 10).

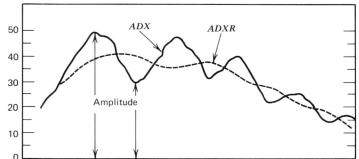

FIGURE 10

The amplitude of the curve is measured from the zero line. The peaks and valleys of the ADX curve indicate a change of direction. If the major trend is down, the peaks would be low price points and the valleys would be high price points. If the major trend is up, the peaks would be high price points and the valleys would be low price points.

The higher the amplitude, the higher is the directional movement in one direction, either up or down, which is indicative of the major trend. The greater the distance between the peaks and valleys, the greater are the reactions to the trend. If the reactions are of significant duration and distance, the trend-following system will be profitable in both directions.

The *ADXR* must be indicative of good directional movement, but it must not overly fluctuate at equilibrium points. This is achieved by taking the average of a 14-day differential of the *ADX*.

Now that we have determined the *ADXR* to be the factor that rates the trending characteristics of a commodity, let's look at the other three factors that make up the commodity selection index.

First, *Volatility:* Volatility is also an indicator of movement. The paradox is that volatility is always accompanied by movement, but movement is not always accompanied by volatility. A commodity can move up very slowly and be high on the *ADXR*, but still be low on the volatility index.

For this reason, the most important index to use for a trend-following system is the *ADXR;* however, the most money is generally made in the shortest period of time when the stock or commodity is volatile. Those who don't like the risk associated with volatile markets should stay with the *ADXR* and trade the commodities on the higher end of the scale which suit their inclinations and pocketbooks.

For those who have the capital and are looking for the best overall situation, the commodity selection index (*CSI*) equation takes in all of the following factors:

1. Directional movement
2. Volatility
3. Margin requirement
4. Commission costs

The factors are individually weighted in the order listed above. The *commodity selection index equation* is:

$$CSI = ADXR \times ATR_{14} \left[\frac{V}{\sqrt{M}} \times \frac{1}{150 + C} \right] \times 100$$

where $ADXR$ = Average directional movement index rating
       ATR_{14} = 14-day average true range
            (The ATR_{14} is the TR_{14} as discussed previously, divided by 14)
       V = Value of a 1¢ move (or the basic increment of the ATR_{14} in dollars)
       M = Margin requirement in dollars $\sqrt{M}$ = square root of M
       C = Commission in dollars

NOTE: *The result of the term 1/(150 + C) must be carried to four decimal places*

Now let's look at an extreme example.

Suppose the factors for two commodities are as follows:

	ADXR	**ATR**$_{14}$	**M**	**C**	**V**
Soybeans	50	15¢	$3000	$45	$ 50
Pork Bellies	37	1.7¢	$1500	$60	$360

Substituting in the equation for *soybeans:*

$$CSI = 50 \times 15.00 \left[\frac{50}{\sqrt{3000}} \times \frac{1}{150 + 45} \right] \times 100$$

$$= 50 \times 15.00 \left[\frac{50}{54.77} \times \frac{1}{195} \right] \times 100$$

$$= 50 \times 15.00 \times .91 \times .0051 \times 100$$

$$= 348 \text{ (for soybeans)}$$

Substituting in the equation for *pork bellies:*

$$CSI = 37 \times 1.70 \left[\frac{360}{\sqrt{1500}} \times \frac{1}{150 + 60} \right] \times 100$$

$$= 37 \times 1.70 \left[\frac{360}{38.73} \times \frac{1}{210} \right] \times 100$$

$$= 37 \times 1.70 \times 9.30 \times .0048 \times 100$$

$$= 280 \text{ (for pork bellies)}$$

Therefore, soybeans has the higher rating of the two.

Now let's look again at the *CSI* equation and point out a short cut that can be used. All the values inside the brackets are *constant* as long as the margin requirement and the commission cost do not change. The 100 is also a constant.

The equation then, can be rewritten so that K represents all of the constants:

$$CSI = ADXR \times ATR_{14} \times K$$

We can therefore calculate K one time for each commodity being followed and use that value every day multiplied by the $ADXR$ and the ATR_{14} to obtain the CSI for that day. We only have to recalculate K when and if either the margin requirement changes or the commission rate changes.

In the previous *CSI* equation for *soybeans:*

$$CSI = 50 \times 15.00 \left[\frac{50}{\sqrt{3000}} \times \frac{1}{150 + 45} \right] \times 100$$

$$
\begin{aligned}
K &= \left[\frac{50}{\sqrt{3000}} \times \frac{1}{150 + 45} \right] \times 100 \\
&= \quad .91 \quad \times \quad .0051 \quad \times 100 \\
&= \quad .4641
\end{aligned}
$$

$$
\begin{aligned}
\text{Therefore, } CSI &= ADXR \times ATR_{14} \times K \\
&= \quad 50 \ \times \ 15 \ \times \ .4641 \\
&= \quad 348
\end{aligned}
$$

For *pork bellies:*

$$
\begin{aligned}
K &= \left[\frac{360}{\sqrt{1500}} \times \frac{1}{150 + 60} \right] \times 100 \\
&= \quad 9.30 \quad \times \quad .0048 \quad \times 100 \\
&= \quad 4.464
\end{aligned}
$$

$$
\begin{aligned}
\text{Therefore, } CSI &= ADXR \times ATR_{14} \times K \\
&= \quad 37 \ \times \ 1.70 \ \times \ 4.464 \\
&= \quad 280
\end{aligned}
$$

The ATR_{14} is the value of the *ATR* divided by 14.

To obtain the *CSI* for each day, simply multiply $ADXR \times ATR_{14} \times K$.

Now let's look at another extreme example.

Suppose coffee is highest on the *ADXR* at 70 and the *volatility index* shows that its average true range (ATR_{14}) is 3.75¢.

At $375.00 for a 1¢ move, the average dollar movement per day is 3.75 × 375 = $1,406.25. This seems good so far, but if the margin requirement is $9,000 per contract and the commission is $85.00, then how does coffee compare with trading soybeans in the previous example? The factors are as follows:

	ADXR	ATR_{14}	*M*	*C*	*V*
Soybeans	50	15¢	$3000	$45	$ 50
Coffee	70	3.75¢	$9000	$85	$375

For coffee: $CSI = 70 \times 3.75 \left[\dfrac{375}{\sqrt{9000}} \times \dfrac{1}{150 + 85} \right] \times 100$

$\qquad = 70 \times 3.75 \left[\dfrac{375}{94.87} \times \dfrac{1}{235} \right] \times 100$

$\qquad = 70 \times 3.75 \times \quad 3.95 \quad \times \quad .0043 \quad \times 100$

$\qquad = \quad 318 \text{ (for coffee)}$

The *CSI* for soybeans was 348; therefore, soybeans is the better overall selection.

Now let's analyze the soybean situation:

The average true range (ATR_{14}) is 15¢ $\times$ 50.00 = \$750 average dollar movement per day. This is only about half that of coffee, and in addition, soybeans has less directional movement than coffee.

To give you an idea of what the *CSI* equation does, let's make two general suppositions; let's say that we traded both coffee and soybeans:

1. Suppose we got 70% of the move in coffee since *ADXR* for coffee was 70, the same reasoning would give us 50% of the soybean move.

2. Suppose we are in each trade for 10 days, so that our money is tied up for the same period of time.

For coffee:

$$\begin{array}{lr} \text{\$1406.25 per day for 10 days} \times 70\% = & \$9,843.75 \\ \text{Less commission} & 85.00 \\ \hline \text{Profit} & \$9,758.75 \end{array}$$

For soybeans:

$$\begin{array}{lr} \text{\$750 per day for 10 days} \times 50\% = & \$3,750.00 \\ \text{Less commission} & 45.00 \\ \hline \text{Profit} & \$3,705.00 \end{array}$$

However, because of the difference in margin requirement, we could have traded three contracts of soybeans for *each* contract of coffee; therefore, 3 $\times$ \$3,705 = \$11,115.

The profit on soybeans was $\qquad\qquad$ \$11,115.00
The profit on coffee was $\qquad\qquad\quad$ 9,758.75

The *commodity selection index* for soybeans was $\qquad$ 348
The *commodity selection index* for coffee was $\qquad$ 318

$\qquad\qquad\qquad\qquad\qquad\qquad\qquad$ 30 ÷ 318 = 9%

The *ADXR* indicated that soybeans was a 9% better choice than coffee. Actually, in the example soybeans was a 13.9% better choice than coffee.

$$\begin{array}{r} \$11,115.00 \\ - \quad 9,758.75 \\ \hline \$ \ 1,356.25 \ \div \ 9758.75 \ = \ 13.9\% \end{array}$$

I realize that what we are dealing with here is not an exact science. The margin requirements will not be set, nor could they be set to maintain a constant relationship with volatility or directional movement, nor any other variable, for that matter. There is, however, a direct—though not constant—relationship between margin requirement, volatility and directional movement. The *CSI* equation constantly analyzes all of these factors and points out the most advantageous situations.

As a rule, margin requirements lag market action. They are slow to go up and slow to go down. The *commodity selection index* also enables the trader to take advantage of this lag to obtain the best return on invested capital.

Most technical systems are trend-following systems; however, most commodities are in a good trending mode (high directional movement) only about 30% of the time. *If the trader follows the same commodities or stocks all of the time, then his system has to be good enough to make more money 30% of the time than it will give back 70% of the time. Compare that approach to trading only the top five or six commodities on the CSI scale.*

This is the concept of selection and direction. Use your own trend-following system or method for entering and exiting the market and trade the commodities which are highest on the Commodity Selection Index.

Dr. Charles J. Testa is president of Infosystems Technology, Inc., a privately held corporation in Falls Church, Virginia, providing consulting and computer-based financial management services to a wide variety of clients. His background includes an MS in business administration, a PhD in biotechnology (both from UCLA), and an illustrious career in teaching, consulting, and basic research in operations analysis and data base management. He is in wide demand as a speaker and has authored numerous articles on the effective design, implementation, and utilization of information systems.

Dr. Michael B. Hargrove earned his PhD in economics at the University of Kentucky in 1971. He has over 10 years of both theoretical and practical experience in the application of Box–Jenkins, time series, and regression techniques in designing forecasting models for everything from freight-car demand to the price structure of the world's foodstuffs, metals, and fibers. His work has appeared in a wide variety of professional journals and seminars.

The formal analysis of commodity price movement is still in its infancy when compared to the applications of Markov chains, Fourier, and spectral analyses which have been applied to the securities markets. Although some work done in securities can be used for commodities, the following paper represents a new effort aimed directly at commodities.

The most familiar form of technical analysis is the moving average, which has been used to evaluate securities price trends for many years. Moving averages are in the category *of* time-series analysis, *since they are based on a continuous series of price data. Most time-series analyses are assumed to identify market trends with a certain degree of error, considered a random-error component. This concept is familiar to those who have studied the decomposition of price movement using econometrics. When you take the primary characteristics out of price movement—the trend, cycle, and seasonality—you are left with the last component: an unpredictable, random element. During analysis, it is common that all price movement is considered a sequence of independent random variables. Sometimes, the three non-random components are extracted and only the fourth element is assumed to be entirely random and analyzed as such.*

The assumption of independent random variables may be a pure approach to forecasting, but it may also be unnecessary. There are many cases in which the sequential elements in a time series are highly dependent. It would be inefficient to apply a solution that did not take advantage of all the available information. The work of G. E. Box and G. M. Jenkins has been the basis of forecasting models that assume measurable properties of these "random variables." The following article by Charles J. Testa and Michael Hargrove introduces the use of Box–Jenkins methods in commodities.

THE BOX-JENKINS APPROACH TO COMMODITY FORECASTS

CHARLES J. TESTA

MICHAEL HARGROVE

The "random-walk" description of stock and commodity price behavior is a controversial—and often confusing—issue. But practitioners as well as scholars have come to recognize its importance. It has even spawned a best seller—*A Random Walk Down Wall Street*, by professor Burton Malkiel, an eminent economic advisor.

The random-walk issue boils down to one basic question: Are the price and volume news printed daily in newspapers useful for predicting future price movements? Those who support the random-walk model say "No!"

Evidence supporting the random walk does not mean that price changes are uncaused. Price changes result from the combined actions of buyers and sellers that shift the market's equilibrium between demand and supply. For example, when the demand for a commodity increases, relative to its supply, this imbalance causes a price rise that is sufficient to attract sellers who restore the market to economic equilibrium.

Since price changes are caused by changes in either the net supply or demand for investments, above-average investing strategies can be developed if one can:

1. Determine what causes people to change their minds.
2. Act on this information before it is fully reflected in the price of the investment.

This logical approach to achieving above-average rates of return introduces the issue of the efficient capital market theory.

The Efficient Capital Market Theory

The setting for an efficient capital market is a market in which many people, with similar investment objectives and access to the same information, actively compete. The stock market certainly provides this setting. Many people—both professionally and privately—continually search for undervalued securities. Also, in their quest for wealth, investors have similar basic objectives. Everyone prefers a high rate of return to a low one, certainty to uncertainty, and so forth. Furthermore, the law requires that both parties in a securities transaction have access to the same material facts.

Scholars have hypothesized that in such a market setting—with many people playing the same game and having similar objectives and equal access to information—it would be impossible for any investor to have a consistent advantage over the market, which reflects the composite judgment of its millions of participants. This hypothesis is known as the efficient capital market theory or the fair-game theory. "Efficient" means that the market is capable of quickly digesting new information on the economy, an industry, or the value of an enterprise, and accurately impounding that information into the price of the stock. "Fair game" means that participants in such markets cannot expect to earn more, or less, than the average return for the risks involved.

The efficient capital market theory hypothesizes that all available information is continually analyzed by some among the literally millions of investors. It holds that in this kind of market for example, news of an earnings increase is quickly and accurately assessed by the combined actions of investors and immediately reflected in the price of the stock.

The purported result of this efficiency is that whether you buy the stock before, during, or after the earnings news or whether you buy another stock, you can expect a fair market rate of return commensurate with the risk of owning whatever security you buy.

It is important to note that this theory might be true for one kind of information, say, earnings, but might not be true for other types of information, such as dividend changes. Similarly, it might hold true for information on particular instruments, say, widely held stocks, or in certain markets, such as the New York Stock Exchange, but not for other instruments or markets such as commodities. Thus when you refer to the efficient capital market theory, you must specify the "information," the "instrument," and the "market."

The efficient capital market theory focuses our search for useful market predictors on that information which might cause people to change their minds about investment values. Thus the theory is a useful guide. From its perspective, researchers can determine which information is "efficiently" and "inefficiently" processed by competing investors in various markets and for various investment instruments. They can hypothesize cause-and-effect relationships and study how efficiently a particular security and market digest a particular kind of information.

Investors tend to focus on one market (NYSE securities), one instrument (common stock), and one or two categories of news items (earnings and dividends). It is likely, therefore, that other fruitful areas exist where investor information processing is *not* efficient. Those who can discover and accurately assess these inefficiencies can profit from their differential knowledge. But because such unrecognized knowledge is disseminated among competing investors, its value to users is destroyed by the equalizing forces of an efficient capital market. Even if research can pinpoint news items that are efficiently processed for particular instruments in particular markets, such knowledge enables investors to avoid analyzing this useless, fully discounted information— an important decision in itself.

To consistently attain above-average investment performance, an investor must know the odds that certain information will influence certain investment instruments in certain investment markets in known directions by approximating magnitudes, and must act on the information before other investors do. If this cannot be done, investment analysis becomes an expensive exercise in hopeful thinking! The fact that over

50,000 professional security analysts, brokers, and portfolio managers —not to mention the millions of investors—are all trying to do the same thing makes the game of investing very competitive.

When placed in the context of the efficient capital market theory, the existing research should prompt us to look for useful information by:

1. Specifying the investment "instrument" that interests us (for example, commodities).

2. Defining the "market" to be studied (for example, the New York Mercantile Exchange).

3. Tabulating the kinds of "information" that might affect the value of the investment instrument.

When possibly useful information is placed in this perspective, one can assess how efficiently information is processed. If the information is quickly and accurately impounded into the instrument's price, the market would be deemed economically "efficient." But if for some reason the market does not fully react to a certain kind of news, or reacts slowly, the discovery of this economic "inefficiency" will permit one to profit in excess of a "fair game."

Commodity Trading Systems

Most of the so-called "advanced" techniques for commodity trading can be classified into two broad categories: (1) *time series models* which attempt to capture the dynamic behavior of data and project it into the future and (2) *econometric models* which attempt to model the causal relationship among economic variables and to project the eventual results of the current causal forces at work. The history of application of both techniques shows varied results. Time series analyses have often employed simplistic models with inadequate model identification procedures which often resulted in models of unknown predictive power. Econometric models have typically required large numbers of variables, very complex model estimation procedures, and extensive model maintenance efforts. Such models have had a poor history of providing timely and cost-effective forecasts.[1]

The work of Box and Jenkins has provided a powerful new tool for forecasting. They have developed a class of very flexible and adaptive models along with a comprehensive method of identification of the appropriate model form, which greatly increase the ability to model and forecast using time series data. These models combine the ability of time series techniques to simply and efficiently make short-term projections with the ability to incorporate the information provided by causal variables without incurring excessive model complexity.[2]

Box–Jenkins models have been successfully applied to analyses of a variety of financial instruments.[3] The available studies indicate the potential of Box–Jenkins models to provide short-term forecasts of economic and financial market variables to support investment decisions.

Box–Jenkins Models

The models proposed by Box and Jenkins can be broadly classified into two categories: univariate models and multivariate (transfer function) models. The univariate model is the autoregressive integrated moving-average model (ARIMA) that, like traditional time series analysis, requires only a history of the variable of interest as input information. The multivariate models are of the linear difference equation type and are a logical extension of the distributed lag type of linear model. These multivariate models require a history of both the variable of interest plus one or more leading indicators. However, they provide greater accuracy, since they incorporate the additional information provided by the leading indicators into the forecast.

Logic of Univariate Models

The observed value of a variable of interest, Y_t, a commodity price, for example, is the result of a complex transformation of the present and past values of some large set of "causal" or "information" variables $X_{1t}, \cdots, X_{kt}$, where k represents the number of variables and t represents time.

$$Y_t = f(X_{1t} \cdots X_{kt}, X_{1t\text{-}1} \cdots X_{kt\text{-}1}, X_{1t\text{-}2} \cdots X_{kt\text{-}2}, \cdots) \qquad (1)$$

The econometric approach of attempting to model this function is often defeated by the (1) complexity of the transformation function, (2) the large number of variables involved (k is large), and (3) number of time lags (having significant impacts) which is quite high. An example of the level of complexity involved in attempting to build econometric models is found in the reports on the Federal Reserve–MIT econometric model which contains hundreds of variables and equations.[4]

The univariate Box–Jenkins model would picture that the "information" variables impact the market in a random manner from day to day so that the net effect of the information variables $(X_{1t}, \cdots, X_{kt})$ can be approximated by a 'shock" (ϵ_t) that behaves in a random manner. In some time periods the aggregate "news" is "good" so that the ϵ_t's are positive, but in other times the "news" is "bad," resulting in negative ϵ_t values. The Box–Jenkins model assumes that in the long run, the "news" is neutral so that the expected "shock," $E(\epsilon_t)$, is zero and the size of the period by period "shocks" can be measured by their variance, σ^2. The transformation function is then stated as a linear transformation:

$$Y_t = \epsilon_t + \theta_1 \epsilon_{t-1} + \theta_2 \epsilon_{t-2} + \cdots \qquad (2)$$

where $\theta_1, \theta_2, \cdots$ are weights that represent the aging of past information effects on current values of Y. Equation (2) is a "moving-average" model (MA) form which has been used to match the behavior of economic time series since the 1930s. At time $t-1$, Y_t can be calculated from $Y_{t-1} = \epsilon_{t-1} + \theta_1 \epsilon_{t-2} + \theta_2 \epsilon_{t-3} + \cdots$ Then by transposition ϵ_{t-1} can be expressed as $\epsilon_{t-1} = Y_{t-1} - \theta_1 \epsilon_{t-2} - \theta_2 \epsilon_{t-3} - \cdots$. Substituting in Equation (2) for ϵ_{t-1}, the ϵ_{t-1} term can be replaced by a Y_{t-1} term. Repeating this process for $\epsilon_{t-2}, \epsilon_{t-3}, \cdots$ results in expressing Y_t in terms of its past values, the autoregressive form (AR)

$$Y_t = \phi_1 Y_{t-1} + \phi_2 Y_{t-2} + \cdots \epsilon_t \qquad (3)$$

where $\phi_1, \phi_2, \cdots$ are weights applied to the past values of Y or in the form where Y_t is expressed in terms of both its past values and "shocks," the autoregressive integrated moving average form (ARIMA)

$$Y_t = \phi_1 Y_{t-1} + \phi_2 Y_{t-2} + \cdots + \epsilon_t + \theta_1 \epsilon_{t-1} + \theta_2 \epsilon_{t-2} + \cdots \qquad (4)$$

The first major contribution of Box and Jenkins is the demonstration that any type of time series behavior can be represented by Equation (2) or its equivalent forms given by Equations (3) and (4). Since the models are of infinite order, involving an infinite number of coefficients, to make these models estimatable an appropriate method of finding a model form of finite order to approximate the series behavior is required. The identification process to determine the most parsimonious model—a model with the smallest number of parameters—that adequately reflects the dynamic behavior of the variable of interest is the second major contribution of Box and Jenkins. The model identification process is based on matching the autocorrelation pattern of the observed history of the variable of interest with the known patterns of various specific forms of the ARIMA model. A full discussion of the identification process can be found in several recent works.[5] The typical result of this approach is the development of a relatively simple model structure which captures the dynamic behavior of the data. Examples of successful application of this approach to modeling a variety of time series, including long distance telephone demand,[6] electric power demands,[7] and commodity demand,[8] can be found in the literature.

The univariate approach to time series modeling has the advantages of minimum data requirements and estimation costs, but it has no ability to utilize the sources of information other than the history of the series of interest. This is often a severe limitation in the area of financial forecasting. A second problem with univariate modeling is that if a market is temporally efficient, the model will be found to be

$$Y_t = Y_{t-1} + \epsilon_t$$
$$\text{or}$$
$$Y_t - Y_{t-1} = \epsilon_t \tag{5}$$

which is the widely known random-walk model.[9] To make accurate predictions in temporally efficient markets, more information is necessary than just the history of the series.

Transfer Function Modeling

The multivariate approach to time series analysis developed by Box and Jenkins is called transfer function analysis. The transfer function is designed to model the dynamics of the impact of changes in one or more causal variables X on the variable of interest Y. This type of model allows the forecasting of results of changes in important information variables.

Before 1971 exchange rates were generally fixed and businessmen only had to worry about occasional devaluations. During 1971, however, one currency after another was allowed to "float" against the dollar, with supply and demand determining its value in United States dollars. There was an attempt in late 1971, in the so-called Smithsonian agreement, to fix new rates, but these fell apart. At this time currencies generally are floating, although governments intervene in the market to prevent too precipitous a fall or rise. With the exchange rates of some currencies often erratic and with nations' central banks often intervening, anyone in this area is-dealing in perhaps the roughest market in the world. The application of transfer function models to this area is intriguing, to say the least.

For example, let Y_t be the spot price of the British pound and X_t be the ratio of internal inflation rates between the United States and Great Britain. Then, a transfer function model, using hypothetical constants, can be expressed as

$$(1-.93B)\,Y_t = \frac{(1-.12B)}{(1-.08B)}\, X_t + (1+.32B)\epsilon_t$$

where B is the backshift operator such that $BY_t = Y_{t-1}$. After the appropriate calculations, the final model form would be

$$Y_t - 1.01\ Y_{t-1} + .075\ Y_{t-2} = X_t - .12X_{t-1} + \epsilon_t + .24\epsilon_{t-1} - .025\epsilon_{t-2}$$

Hypothetically, this would suggest that a 1% increase in the inflation rate ratio would result in a $.96\%$ increase in the spot price of the British pound.

As in the case of univariate modeling, the major contributions of Box and Jenkins are (1) to demonstrate that virtually all types of dynamic response can be modeled by the use of linear difference equations and (2) to develop an identification procedure to determine the specific model whose dynamic response matches the response between the particular output and input variables of interest. The identification procedure for transfer function models is considerably more complex than that for univariate models.

An example of the application of transfer function methodology to a financial analysis conducted by the authors is a study of the time dynamics of the reaction of option prices on the CBOE to changes in the related stock prices on the NYSE. The option valuation model of Black–Scholes has established the theoretical importance of the related stock price in determining option prices, but the dynamics of the adjustment process might give investment opportunities if the adjustment process is lagged.

Five option-stock series were modeled over a 9-month period, September 1974 to June 1975, with the results given in Table 1.

TABLE 1 DISCRETE LINEAR TRANSFER FUNCTION MODELS OF DYNAMIC RELATIONSHIP BETWEEN OPTION MARKET PRICE (Y_t) AND FORMULA VALUE (X_t)

Series	Model	Impulse at Lags				Gain
		0	**1**	**2**	**3**	**Gain**
AT&T April–45	$(1-0.1028B)(1-B)Y_t =$ $0.6006(1-B)X_t + a_t$	0.6006	0.0617	0.0063	0.0006	0.6694
AT&T July–45	$(1-0.0917B)(1-B)Y_t =$ $0.5658(1-B)X_t + a_t$	0.5658	0.0519	0.0046	0.0004	0.6229
Avon April–30	$(1-0.1460B(1-B)Y_t =$ $0.7838(1-B)X_t + \dfrac{.1}{1+0.41B}a_t$	0.7838	0.1144	0.0167	0.0024	0.9178
Kodak April –80	$(1-0.0375B)(1-B)Y_t =$ $0.8454(1-B)X_t + a_t$	0.8454	0.0317	0.0012	0.0001	0.8783
Polaroid April–20	$(1-0.0934B)(1-B)Y_t =$ $0.8449(1-B)X_t + a_t$	0.8449	0.0789	0.0073	0.0007	0.9319

With the identification procedures of Box and Jenkins, simple, first-order transfers were found to characterize the dynamic response in all series. The gain values, the response in option price in the ith period to a \$1 change in stock price show that the adjustment in option prices occurs rapidly, with 90% or more of the eventual adjustment occurring with zero lag (within the same trading day).

This particular analysis does not lend to the development of profitable investment strategies, since the adjustment to the information input is too rapid to allow the making of profitable trades. This analysis does show the ability of the Box–Jenkins transfer procedure to identify simple, accurate models to dynamically relate information variables to security price actions. The realization of the nature of the relationships in this situation avoids the wasting of time and effort in attempting to develop investment strategies in a situation where no potential exists.

Models of Reflecting Barriers

The investment literature suggests that many financial series obey a random-walk discipline except when they enter price regions where they exhibit a reflecting behavior; that is, the pattern of day-to-day fluctuations exhibits a systematic trend until it moves outside the barrier region. The existence of such regions is justified through the logical actions of professional investors when the random actions of small investors have moved the market price to distinctly "underpriced" or "overpriced" areas.

Very profitable investment strategies are available to the investor who is aware of the nonrandom price changes to be expected in the barrier area. The problem from the investor's point of view is to determine the existence of a reflecting barrier and to determine the price boundaries of the region. Transfer function models are capable of modeling the reflecting barrier behavior of a financial series through the use of an intervention variable that indicates the movement into a barrier region.[10] The intervention model can be used both to test for the existence of a reflecting barrier and to model the dynamic behavior of the price series in the barrier region.

Summary

The Box–Jenkins procedures discussed in this paper are the optimum means for short- to intermediate-term forecasting. They combine the relative simplicity of time series analysis with powerful identification and evaluation procedures. In the multivariate form they allow optimum use of the information provided by leading indicators without resulting to the complexities of simultaneous equation models.

The Box–Jenkins approach is a data-directed model-development procedure designed to discover the minimum model adequate to explain the dynamic behavior of the variables of interest rather than developing large and complex models. As a result, the costs associated with collecting and analyzing data, constructing the model, developing computer programs, and testing and validating the model are usually less than those for econometric models.

References

1. G. H. Moore, "Forecasting Short-Run Change," *Journal of the American Statistical Association, 64* (March 1969) 1–22.
   H. V. Steckler, "Forecasting With Econometric Models: An Evaluation," *Econometrica, 36* (1969) 437–463.

V. Zarnowitz, *An Appraisal of Short-Term Economic Forecasts*, (New York: National Bureau of Economic Research, 1967).

2. G. E. P. Box and G. M. Jenkins, *Time Series Analysis: Forecasting and Control, 2nd Edition* (San Francisco: Holden Day) 1976.

   J. C. Chambers, S. K. Mullich, and D. D. Smith, "How to Choose the Right Forecasting Technique," *Harvard Business Review, 49* (July–August 1971) 45–74.

   C. R. Nelson, *Applied Time-Series Analysis for Managerial Forecasting* (San Francisco: Holden Day, 1973) 202–221.

3. R. J. Rugalski, "Bond Yields: Trends or Random Walks?", *Decision Sciences, 6* (January 1976) 666–669.

   R. Ball and R. Watts, "Some Time Series Properties of Accounting Income," *Journal of Finance, 27* (June 1972) 662–681.

   J. C. McKeown and K. S. Lorsk, "A Comparative Analysis of the Predictive Ability of Adaptive Forecasting, Re-Estimation, and Re-Identification Using Box–Jenkins Time Series Analysis on Quarterly Earnings Data," *Decision Sciences, 9* (October 1976) 655–672.

   V. A. Mabert and R. C. Radcliffe, "A Forecasting Methodology as Applied to Financial Time Series," *The Accounting Review, 49* (January 1974) 61–75.

4. F. deLewn and F. Gramlich, "The Federal Reserve-MIT Econometric Model," *Federal Reserve Bulletin, 54* (January 1964) 11–40.

5. T. W. Ferrat and V. A. Mabert, "A Description and Application of the Box–Jenkins Methodology," *Decision Sciences, 3* (October 1972) 93–107.

   Nelson, *op. cit.* pp. 30–201.

6. G. C. Tiao and H. E. Thompson, "Analysis of Telephone Data: A Case Study Forecasting Seasonal Time Series," *The Bell Journal of Economics and Management Science, 2* (Fall 1971) 515–541.

7. Ferratt and Mabert, *op. cit.* 99–104.

8. G. C. Tiao and P. J. Pack, "Modeling the Consumption of Frozen Orange Juice: A Case Study of Time Series Analysis," *Technical Report 228* (Madison: Department of Statistics, University of Wisconsin, 1970).

   R. M. Leuthold et al., "Forecasting of Daily Hog Prices and Quantities: A Study of Alternative Forecasting Techniques," *Journal of the American Statistical Association, 65* (March 1970) 90–107.

9. E. F. Fama, "Random Walks in Stock Market Prices," *Financial Analysts Journal* (September–October 1965) 3–7.

10. For a discussion of Transfer Function Modeling and qualitative "Interventions," see G. E. P. Box and G. C. Tiao, "Intervention Analysis with Applications to Economic and Environmental Problems," *Journal of the American Statistical Association, 70* (December 1975) 1–70.

PART 3

ANALYTICAL METHODS

Conventional wisdom tells us that the higher prices are, the more they fluctuate. A 10¢ move in $3.00 soybeans, for example, is the same percentage *fluctuation as a 30¢ move in $9.00 beans.*

As for most conventional wisdom, however, there is more than meets the eye in the relationship of prices and price volatility. In addition to the absolute level of prices, the time interval over which price variation is measured and the effect of inflation must also be considered.

P. J. Kaufman begins with the assumption that there is a positive correlation among the price level, the time interval for measurement, and price volatility. He then shows you how this relationship can be verified, using the soybean oil futures market as his example.

The result is a set of equations that form the basis for analysis of other markets that might differ in their liquidity or sensitivity to inflation. The purpose of the research is not to yield a trading "system" to generate instant profits but to add an important facet to the understanding of price behavior and how the price–volatility relationship might be exploited within larger algorithms.

THE PRICE-VOLATILITY RELATIONSHIP IN COMMODITIES

PERRY J. KAUFMAN

Before complex price theories and mathematical models can be developed, it is essential that each aspect of price movement and each behavioral characteristic of price patterns be studied independently. By understanding the basic components of price movement, more sophisticated theories can be developed which use these elements correctly and without duplication. By decomposing price movement using known, reliable techniques, the residual patterns should be more applicable to analysis.

The *price–volatility relationship* is one of the basic characteristics of price movement. It is founded on the simplest observation of price fluctuations which can be seen on any chart: fluctuations increase as price increases. It is reasonable to assume that there is more latitude for fluctuation as prices increase; the value of gold at $35 per ounce may vary by a few dollars a year, but at $200 per ounce it will fluctuate up to $40 and still be considered "normal."

Another obvious relationship is that the potential for price variation will increase as the time interval used for measurement increases. If

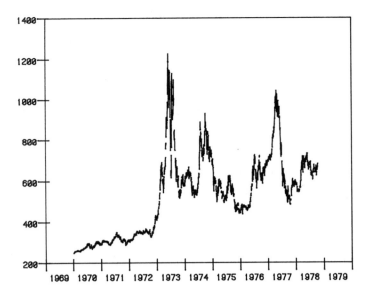

FIGURE 1
Cash #1 yellow soybeans, Chicago.

volatility (the difference between the highest and lowest prices) is measured over one week, it will be substantially greater than the volatility of only one day. The volatility is expected to increase rapidly while the interval increases from one day to one month, but as the interval continues to increase in size the corresponding volatility should reach a maximum and level off. Any time interval that exceeds the duration of the maximum price fluctuation will not show a corresponding increase in volatility. Figure 1 shows a price chart of cash soybeans for a 9-year period; it is easy to see that the price fluctuations were small from 1970 through 1972. At the peak of 1973 the volatility increased dramatically. In Figure 1 we can see that the greatest price fluctuations occurred in less than a 1-year span, from late 1972 to mid-1973; consequently, any increase in the measurement interval greater than this duration will not reflect increased peak volatility.

We start out studying the price–volatility relationship by assuming that there is some positive correlation among the price level, time interval for measurement, and potential price fluctuations. There are important advantages in finding a uniform relationship. First, we would know the likelihood of a potential move over a specific time period. This could be used to identify the risk of carrying cash or futures positions at different price levels. Contrarily, an abnormally large price fluctuation could be identified and countered; that is, a sharp movement down that reaches or exceeds the probable limits could be used as a purchasing opportunity. In addition, the volatility relationship could be used to balance the risks of a diversified portfolio or to define a risk-to-reward ratio of profit potential. It serves as a guide for what is normal or expected at each price level.

Method of Measurement

Volatility is the variation in price over a specific interval. A simple approach to measurement would be to take the maximum price fluctuation over an interval related to the average daily price during the same period. The result would be a measurement of extreme price variation. Although this relationship can be formalized, there is still a problem in determining the likelihood that the extreme will be reached. The results do not allow for distinguishing different levels of probable movement.

Instead of using extreme variation, the distribution of the closing prices of a specified interval will be analyzed with respect to its variation from the mean price of the interval. This variation can be expressed as a standard deviation and used to explain potential price fluctuations as probabilities. Although the ultimate relationship between price and volatility may be the same as with extreme price movement, the results are more useful when presented in terms of standard deviations from the mean.

The intervals selected for this test will range from 1 month to 11 months. It is expected that intervals smaller or larger than this range will show a limiting condition. The smaller ranges will severely contain price movement, and the larger ranges will not show corresponding increases in volatility.

Testing of Raw Data

Using a computer program developed to test the price–volatility relationship, we can produce the necessary averages and standard deviations for varying intervals. The futures markets will be used, since the data is most readily available. The primary study will use soybean oil, selected deliveries, since it is representative of a liquid market; we will

TABLE 1   ANALYSIS OF PRICE DEVIATION BY CONTRACT, BEGINNING WITH CONTRACT JULY 1969—SOYBEAN OIL, 3-MONTH INTERVALS

P J KAUFMAN COMMODITIES RESEARCH   03/22/79

ANALYSIS OF PRICE DEVIATION BY CONTRACT

BEGINNING WITH CONTRACT JUL69 SOYBEAN OIL

3 MONTH INTERVALS, STORED IN RECORD   3

	CONTR	END	DAYS	AVG	STDEV
1	(SON69)	2-69	61	829	13.12
2	(SON69)	5-69	61	828	19.68
3	(SON70)	2-70	60	906	55.14
4	(SON70)	5-70	63	1065	65.23
5	(SON71)	2-71	61	1173	38.01
6	(SON71)	5-71	64	1128	45.30
7	(SON72)	2-72	62	1143	29.98
8	(SON72)	5-72	64	1182	31.91
9	(SON73)	2-73	59	1121	144.75
10	(SON73)	5-73	64	1521	136.69
11	(SON74)	2-74	59	2189	307.52
12	(SON74)	5-74	64	2509	200.38
13	(SON75)	2-75	62	3074	333.64
14	(SON75)	5-75	63	2469	200.91
15	(SON76)	2-76	61	1689	64.18
16	(SON76)	5-76	64	1659	49.13
17	(SON77)	2-77	61	2233	91.15
18	(SON77)	5-77	63	2925	208.27
19	(SON78)	2-78	61	2092	56.77
20	(SON78)	5-78	64	2598	126.80
21	(SOZ69)	8-69	63	724	12.63
22	(SOZ69)	11-69	63	884	95.46
23	(SOZ70)	8-70	65	1007	28.11
24	(SOZ70)	11-70	62	1201	127.27
25	(SOZ71)	8-71	65	1256	75.51
26	(SOZ71)	11-71	63	1253	43.47
27	(SOZ72)	8-72	65	1023	28.60
28	(SOZ72)	11-72	62	981	30.29
29	(SOZ73)	8-73	63	1754	311.69
30	(SOZ73)	11-73	63	1835	277.56
31	(SOZ74)	8-74	64	3105	579.20
32	(SOZ74)	11-74	62	4026	367.10
33	(SOZ75)	8-75	64	2208	286.89
34	(SOZ75)	11-75	63	2086	208.98
35	(SOZ76)	8-76	65	2043	157.83
36	(SOZ76)	11-76	62	2199	112.99
37	(SOZ77)	8-77	65	2220	304.42
38	(SOZ77)	11-77	63	1914	129.52
39	(SOZ78)	8-78	65	2281	101.20
40	(SOZ78)	11-78	62	2505	84.80

also use nonoverlapping test periods, so that each contract will be tested for the months just prior to delivery.

The soybean oil contracts were tested for time intervals of 1, 2, 3, 6, and 11 months for the years 1969–1978. Prior to 1972, prices were steadier at lower levels and the additional data may not have affected the results significantly. Later tests show that the assumption is correct. Table 1 shows the raw data calculations for 3-month intervals of oil. Each contract is used for six months of prices: December through May for July delivery and June through November for December delivery. The prices are analyzed by taking the average over the interval (column 5) and the standard deviation of prices over the same interval (column 6). These calculations form data sets that are then evaluated for four unique regression analyses: linear, exponential, power, and logarithmic.

$$
\begin{aligned}
\text{linear:} \quad & V = A + B \cdot P \\
\text{exponential:} \quad & \ln V = \ln A + B \cdot P \\
\text{power:} \quad & \ln V = \ln A + B \cdot \ln P \\
\text{logarithmic:} \quad & V = A + B \cdot \ln P
\end{aligned}
$$

where V is the volatility (dependent on the standard deviation variable),
$\quad$ P is the average price,
$\quad$ A is the V intercept, and
$\quad$ B is the slope.

Analysis of Results

The results of the tests show that the power fit best represents the nature of the price–volatility relationship with a relatively good correlation. Equations for power and linear regressions are shown in Table 2.

TABLE 2   POWER FIT AND LINEAR REGRESSION EQUATIONS

Interval	Power Fit	Linear Regression
1 month	$\ln V = -9.350 + 1.805 \ln P$, $R = .825$	$V = -49.26 + .074P$, $R = .704$
2 months	$\ln V = -9.441 + 1.864 \ln P$, $R = .853$	$V = -58.196 + .097P$, $R = .743$
3 months	$\ln V = -8.607 + 1.774 \ln P$, $R = .804$	$V = -71.683 + .119P$, $R = .787$
6 months	$\ln V = -8.416 + 1.805 \ln P$, $R = .808$	$V = -133.78 + .189P$, $R = .874$
11 months	$\ln V = -3.629 + 1.231 \ln P$, $R = .792$	$V = -114.1 + .235P$, $R = .691$

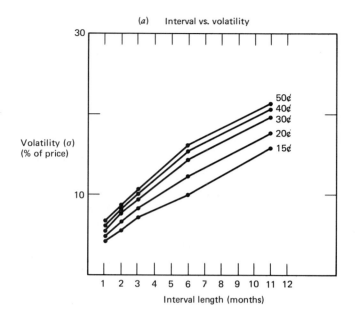

(a)   Interval vs. volatility

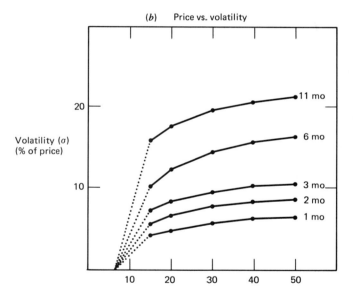

(b)   Price vs. volatility

FIGURE 2
Soybean oil price—volatility relationships.
(a) Interval vs. volatility.
(b) Price vs. volatility.

104

Since it is easier to visualize a linear relationship, the analysis of the formulas will be performed on those equations. It should be noted that the correlation coefficients were reasonably high for both power and linear regressions, and there is similar uniformity in the coefficients in both sets of equations.

The simplest way to evaluate the results is by plotting the volatility against both the price and the interval length. We can then visualize the changes that occur when one or the other is varied. Figure 2 shows the results when the volatility, calculated from the previous equations, is expressed as a percentage of price. In Figure 2*a* it can be seen that the volatility increases as either the interval or the price level increases. Since it seems that the increasing prices cause the lines to get closer together, Figure 2*b* is replotted to show the relationships of volatility to price. It can easily be seen that the volatility is increasing at a slower rate as the interval increases from 1 to 11 months; in addition, the volatility reaches a high level quickly and stabilizes. This latter feature is generally anticipated, but the initial increase from the base price at 6¢ (volatility of 0) to the first 15¢ volatility level is extremely sharp, and the following change in volatility is surprisingly small. To determine the reasonableness of these results we will first consider the price–volatility relationship theoretically.

Anticipated Price–Volatility Relationship

For short intervals of a few days the magnitude of the volatility is limited by the current exchange daily price range, although in practical application the daily price limit is a more reasonable upper boundary. In Figure 3 we see a conceptualization of the volatility pattern of soybean oil as it relates to a sustained move of the daily price limit.

Continued limit moves, without a break, become increasingly unlikely. The actual curve can be formed by tallying the number of sequences of limit moves that have one or more, two or more, three or more, and so on, limits in a row; the curve tops out at the maximum number of limit moves that has historically occurred in oil. From the pattern of the maximum move we can assume that the normal volatility relationship is of the same shape but of smaller magnitude.

There is added complexity in the changing limits as prices increase. It is common for the commodity exchanges to increase the daily price

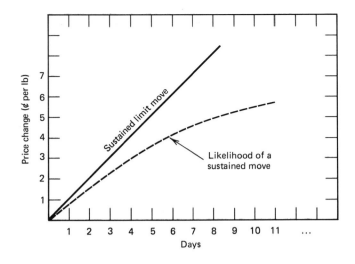

FIGURE 3
Maximum vs. probable price move.

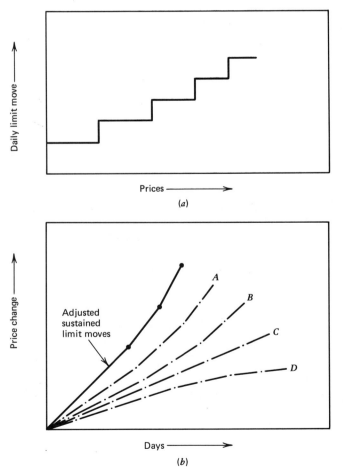

(a)

(b)

FIGURE 4
(a) *Increases in daily price limits.*
(b) *Adjusted maximum vs. probable price movement.*

limits when prices rise to a point where the limits are reached frequently; some exchanges currently allow for automatically expanding limits. In most cases, as represented in Figure 4a, limits expand in a stepped manner. This change will alter the pattern of Figure 3 by increasing the slope of the sustained limit move line incrementally at higher price levels. Figure 4b shows what is expected of the upper bound for volatility over varying intervals, related to the adjusted sustained limit move.

Figure 4b shows the probable movement lines, indicated by the letters A through D, where A represents the volatility over the shortest interval and D represents the longest interval. It is more likely that the price movements of shorter intervals will approach the maximum bound than the movements over longer intervals. The relationship is comparable to the falling off of the probable movement shown in Figure 3. It should also be noted that the shape of curve A is most closely approximated by a power or exponential regression, and the curve D is more logarithmic, because of its downward shape. Because the transition occurs from A to D, we can reasonably expect some interval to be represented by a linear fit.

If we compare the expected results depicted in Figures 3 and 4 with the actual results shown in Figure 2b, we can see that actual oil results are similar, but not as uniform or smoothly developing as the anticipated results. To correct the problem it is necessary to account for the effects of inflation.

Effects of Inflation on Volatility

If the price chart in Figure 1 is carefully reviewed, it can be seen that the lower price levels have a corresponding lower volatility. It should be expected that there is a substantially low price, below the cost of production, at which there will be no trading activity because there are no more sellers; that point is the *base price* of the commodity. From the equations developed earlier for soybean oil we can calculate the base price for any interval by setting $V = 0$ and solving for P. In the system of linear equations we get base prices of 6.66, 6.00, 6.02, 7.08, and 6.62¢ per pound for the corresponding intervals of 1, 2, 3, 6, and 11 months.

Inflation, which has been exceptionally high in the past few years, will

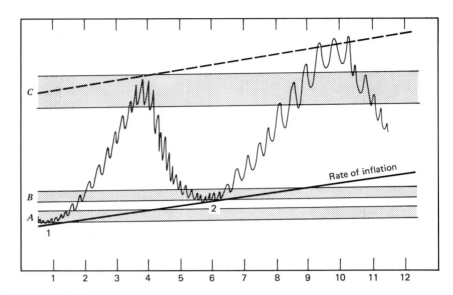

FIGURE 5
Relating volatility and inflation.

cause prices to rise, so that a base price of 6¢ per pound in 1967 should be similar in characteristics to a base price of 12¢ per pound in 1978, where inflation is determined by the government figures for the purchasing power of the United States dollar. We should then expect that, in terms of 1978 dollars, the volatility should near zero at just over 12¢, provided our hypothesis is correct. Figure 5 shows the expected price pattern with respect to inflation.

When prices decline to meet the inflationary line (at points 1 and 2) they become depressed, and volatility drops to a minimum. Since points 1 and 2 occurred six years apart, it is not reasonable to expect the same lows to occur in the sixth year. That would be comparable to soybeans falling to $3.50 per bushel or silver to $2.50 per ounce. According to the diagram there would be no other places to relate the area shown by band *A*, since inflation will prevent prices from returning to that level.

The band described by *B* has a similar problem. In year 1 that price level exhibited increased volatility as prices moved away from the base price, but in year 6 the volatility is lower because the actual price and the base price coincide. Rather than comparing the horizontal band *B*, we should be relating bands that are parallel to the line which represents the rate of inflation.

TABLE 3   PURCHASING POWER OF THE UNITED STATES DOLLAR

	1967	1968	1969	1970	1971	1972	1973	1974	1975	1976	1977	1978
:or	1.000	.960	.911	.860	.821	.798	.752	.678	.621	.587	.549[a]	.503[a]
or	1.988	1.909	1.811	1.710	1.632	1.586	1.495	1.348	1.235	1.167	1.091	1.000

nated.

For practical purposes, an adjustment to prices can be performed by using the inflator shown in Table 3, which has been constructed from the purchasing power of the United States dollar (1967 = 1.000). The inflator is formed simply by dividing all values of the purchasing power by the value of the current year.

The inflator shows that the value of the dollar in 1978 was nearly twice the 1967 value. The approximate value of the inflator for any month can be found by assigning the values in Table 3 to the middle of the year (assume June) and taking the necessary minor increments of value for the months between the middle of one year and the next. This procedure is necessary to avoid any sharp change in value from December to January that would occur if the use of a single inflator value were used for an entire year. We will expect the use of an inflator to correct the problems in Figure 5 by raising the values at point 1 so that they are at the same level as point 2. The corresponding volatility shown in band C should relate closely to other high volatility levels in later years.

Results of Inflating Soybean Oil Prices

When each average monthly soybean oil price is multiplied by the corresponding value of the inflator, we get the results shown in Table 4. This can be compared with Table 1 to see that the column entitled AVG has simply been multiplied by the factor in the column INFLATOR. The standard deviation, which is the measure of volatility, is left alone.

When the regression analysis is again performed on the new data, the power and linear fits are shown in Table 5. In both sets of equations the correlations have become stronger; the base price has expectedly increased to about twice its 1967 level. Using the inflator, the results of all calculations are now in 1978 dollars.

It is now important to look at the price–volatility relationship when the problems of inflation have been discounted. Figure 6 can be compared

TABLE 4 ANALYSIS OF PRICE DEVIATION BY CONTRACT, BEGINNING WITH CONTRACT JULY 1969—SOYBEAN OIL, 3-MONTH INTERVALS

P J KAUFMAN COMMODITIES RESEARCH   03/25/79

ANALYSIS OF PRICE DEVIATION BY CONTRACT

BEGINNING WITH CONTRACT JUL69 SOYBEAN OIL

3 MONTH INTERVALS, STORED IN RECORD 2

	CONTR	END	DAYS	AVG	STDEV	INFLATOR
1	(SON69)	2-69	61	1523	13.12	1.838
2	(SON69)	5-69	61	1500	19.68	1.811
3	(SON70)	2-70	60	1573	55.14	1.737
4	(SON70)	5-70	63	1821	65.23	1.710
5	(SON71)	2-71	61	1939	38.01	1.653
6	(SON71)	5-71	64	1841	45.30	1.632
7	(SON72)	2-72	62	1827	29.98	1.599
8	(SON72)	5-72	64	1876	31.91	1.586
9	(SON73)	2-73	59	1703	144.75	1.520
10	(SON73)	5-73	64	2275	136.69	1.495
11	(SON74)	2-74	59	3038	307.52	1.388
12	(SON74)	5-74	64	3381	200.38	1.348
13	(SON75)	2-75	62	3890	333.64	1.265
14	(SON75)	5-75	63	3048	200.91	1.235
15	(SON76)	2-76	61	2002	64.18	1.185
16	(SON76)	5-76	64	1936	49.13	1.167
17	(SON77)	2-77	61	2484	91.15	1.112
18	(SON77)	5-77	63	3192	208.27	1.091
19	(SON78)	2-78	61	2144	56.77	1.025
20	(SON78)	5-78	64	2598	126.80	1.000
21	(SOZ69)	8-69	63	1298	12.63	1.793
22	(SOZ69)	11-69	63	1561	95.46	1.765
23	(SOZ70)	8-70	65	1707	28.11	1.696
24	(SOZ70)	11-70	62	2012	127.27	1.674
25	(SOZ71)	8-71	65	2039	75.51	1.624
26	(SOZ71)	11-71	63	2019	43.47	1.611
27	(SOZ72)	8-72	65	1605	28.60	1.570
28	(SOZ72)	11-72	62	1516	30.29	1.545
29	(SOZ73)	8-73	63	2576	311.69	1.468
30	(SOZ73)	11-73	63	2621	277.56	1.428
31	(SOZ74)	8-74	64	4122	579.20	1.327
32	(SOZ74)	11-74	62	5220	367.10	1.296
33	(SOZ75)	8-75	64	2699	286.89	1.222
34	(SOZ75)	11-75	63	2512	208.98	1.204
35	(SOZ76)	8-76	65	2356	157.83	1.153
36	(SOZ76)	11-76	62	2491	112.99	1.133
37	(SOZ77)	8-77	65	2386	304.42	1.075
38	(SOZ77)	11-77	63	2009	129.52	1.050
39	(SOZ78)	8-78	65	2224	101.20	0.975
40	(SOZ78)	11-78	62	2380	84.80	0.950

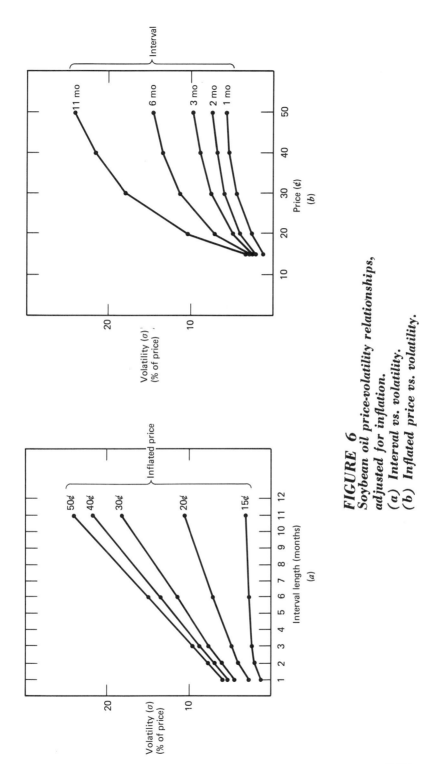

FIGURE 6
Soybean oil price-volatility relationships,
adjusted for inflation.
(a) Interval vs. volatility.
(b) Inflated price vs. volatility.

111

TABLE 5 REGRESSION ANALYSIS—NEW DATA

Interval	Power Fit	Linear Regression	Base Price (¢ per lb)
1 month	$\ln V = -16.19 + 2.617 \ln P, R = .831$	$V = -100.5 + .078P, R = .778$	12.88
2 months	$\ln V = -16.31 + 2.678 \ln P, R = .844$	$V = -115.2 + .098P, R = .782$	11.75
3 months	$\ln V = -16.37 + 2.713 \ln P, R = .840$	$V = -162.6 + .130P, R = .828$	12.50
6 months	$\ln V = -15.88 + 2.702 \ln P, R = .811$	$V = -256.2 + .198P, R = .922$	12.93
11 months	$\ln V = -13.96 + 2.517 \ln P, R = .889$	$V = -449.3 + .330P, R = .919$	13.61

with Figure 2, and it shows considerably more uniformity, closely in line with our theoretical expectations.

Conclusion

This discussion of the price–volatility relationship is not intended to present a perfect set of equations with applications for immediate profits; it is only to show that there are substantial relationships hidden in price data that can be extracted and used to develop various models and systems. The results of an analysis of soybean oil shows that a solid relationship does exist and, when viewed in terms of probable price fluctuation, can be exploited.

Since the relationship of price to volatility is essentially behavioral, it should be consistently strong for most commodities. Variations are a function of two primary factors: the liquidity or control of the market and the relationship of the commodity to inflation itself. In the first case an illiquid market would cause greater dispersion of data points from the mean, reducing the correlation coefficient of the regression analysis. It may be, however, that such extreme movements could be useful for the trader.

The relationship of each commodity to inflation could be seen by performing a regression analysis on a variety of different items, some directly tied to inflation, such as the Swiss franc, treasury bills or gold, and others linked indirectly by export markets, such as wheat or soybean oil. The domestic markets of hogs or potatoes should perform uniquely as well. It can easily be argued that those commodities directly representing inflation-hedging opportunities will be the least volatile relative to both price level and time interval. Treasury bill prices do not fluctuate much because of the arbitrage between other interest rate vehicles; the increase in volatility remains small as prices rise. Because of this phenomenon the Treasury bill patterns may serve as a basis for inflation-level fluctuation for the practical analysis.

As we observe commodities which have increasingly more complex supply-and-demand influences such as gold, we can expect more volatility than treasury bills. Although gold is the basis for many currencies, its use as an inflationary hedge involves a higher degree of behavioral influence than do the United States financial instruments. Crops must be more volatile than any of the financial instruments or precious metals, since they implicitly contain some inflationary factors as well as the uncertainty of supply and demand, transportation, and storage costs. An agricultural product should experience the highest regular level of volatility.

It is then possible to rank the expected volatility of commodities in terms of the number of uncertainties that determine price, once inflation has been eliminated. The United States financial instruments should be ranked the lowest, followed by precious metals and foreign currencies, with agricultural products the greatest. Those products with substantial export markets should be less volatile than domestic markets, since the export serves as an arbitrage by other nations. This application, the evaluation of a practical base price, and the individual price–volatility relationships make this an important concept for the analyst.

R. Earl Hadady *is an electronics engineer. He entered the commodity field in 1971, when he merged his talents with those of James Sibbett. Mr. Sibbett's pioneer work in contrary opinion, begun in 1964, has been carried forth and refined by R. Earl Hadady. Hadady Publications, Inc., an advisory firm, is today recognized as the leading proponent of the application of contrary opinion principles to commodity futures trading.*

The idea of contrary opinion is both understood and accepted on an intuitive level by most traders. Systems which attempt to identify "overbought" or "oversold" price levels are essentially contrary opinion methods, without the opinion. Price analysis often approaches the problem by measurement of distortions or extremes in price movement—once these extremes occur, a directional change or reaction is imminent. Contrary opinion is an analysis of the psychology of the market; it is a polling of the behavioral influences of the traders.

Earl Hadady presents a complete discussion of contrary opinion—its benefits and its problems. His experience in this area is unquestionable and he develops the topic completely. It is important to note that the method is entirely technical, but its use is not well-defined. That is, these are areas where the trader must apply some subjectivity. The lack of a rigid trading signal may be a benefit to the user who is looking for a relative strength index or an added "opinion."

USING CONTRARY OPINION IN THE COMMODITY MARKET

R. EARL HADADY

More than almost any other technical approach,
the premises behind contrary opinion are solidly logical *

You hear a lot about contrary opinion. Brokers use the term, and you frequently see it in market letters. But what is the real significance of contrary opinion? What does it really mean?

Contrary opinion is, in essence, an opinion that is contrary to the majority. And when someone speaks of the use of contrary opinion, he, in general, refers to the fact that he is going contrary to what most people feel the direction of events will be. In the market, therefore, if the majority of the people feel that the prices will rise, the contrarian will be selling and expecting prices to go down. For the purpose of definition in this paper, a contrarian position exists when the majority of the traders in a specific commodity have committed their allocated funds to the same position, either long or short.

* *The Commodity Futures Game*, R. J. Teweles et al. 1974, McGraw Hill Book Company, Inc., New York, p. 199.

The term contrary opinion has been in wide use for many years but it is well understood by relatively few. Humphrey B. Neill, who was the dean of contrary opinion, wrote the bible on the subject *The Art of Contrary Thinking* in 1954. Neill's book dealt with the general subject, but it wasn't until 1964 that James H. Sibbet, an admirer and student of Mr. Neill's, first applied contrary thinking to the commodity futures market. Sibbet devised what he called the "bullish consensus"—a number that measured the degree of bullishness exhibited toward a particular commodity. The basic premise is that when bullishness is at a high level, most bulls have already done their buying and are waiting for prices to move higher. Contrary opinion, of course, states that prices are more likely to go lower, and vice versa. Mr. Sibbet knew he was on to a good thing when the first series of trades, which he called "contrarian," proved to be winners. This success led to the idea of incorporating contrarian trading into a weekly commodity advisory letter, which Mr. Sibbet called *Market Vane*. The letter has been published without interruption since 1964 and is considered the authority on contrary opinion trading.

How and Why Contrary Thinking Works

The principal point about contrary opinion that puzzles many traders is how can most of the traders be bullish if there is a buyer for every seller, as there must be in the commodity market. Analyzing this point and recognizing its significance is the key to really understanding contrary opinion.

Although there is a long position for every short position and vice versa, this does not provide an indication of the actual number of individual traders who are long or short. For example, 90% of the traders in a given commodity can hold 100% of the long positions with only 10% of the traders holding 100% of the short positions. This information provides a very valuable market insight. In the situation cited, the long positions are in "weak" (lightly financed) hands with only one or so contracts held per trader, whereas the short positions are held by relatively few traders. However, the short traders are "strong" hands capable of withstanding financial adversity—rising prices in this example. On the other hand, declining prices can produce a "domino" effect, that is, liquidation by some longs tends to depress prices which in turn produces more liquidations and further depresses prices, and so on. The typical result is a sharp drop in the prices produced by both voluntary and involuntary liquidation of the many weak longs. It is also important to recognize that the well-financed traders, the short side of the market in this case, are not anxious to cover their positions. They have suffered through rising prices, and with the price trend now moving favorably (down) for them, they will hold until they have a substantial profit. The foregoing explains why a contrarian situation usually produces a drastic change in price in a short time—and may be profitable for the contrarian trader.

The reverse situation would be equally applicable, that is, a sharp rise in prices can occur when 90% of the traders are holding short positions and 10% of the traders long positions.

Obtaining a Consensus of Market Opinions Held By Traders

Typically, a consensus on a given subject is obtained in most fields by the use of a market research organization. However, in the commodity field it is relatively easy to determine the consensus, because most commodity futures traders end up losing. As a result of mounting losses, most traders soon abandon their own methods of trading and seek out the advice of professional market analysts. To quantify the consensus, therefore, it is only necessary to determine what the analysts are recommending and the relative number of traders who follow their advice.

Obviously, more traders follow the advice of analysts of the very large brokerage firms than analysts of the smaller firms. The number of clients a brokerage firm has is estimated by first establishing the number of brokers the firm employs. Knowing that a single broker can only handle so many clients, the average number of clients a broker has can then be estimated. It should be borne in mind that it is the number of clients that is important, not the dollar value of the business being transacted. The number of traders following independent market analysts who publish advisory letters is simply related to their number of subscribers.

As of the date of this writing, there are approximately 100 widely read and distributed sources for professional commodity trading recommendations. Most of these sources publish or provide their recommendations at the end of the week, which makes it convenient and timely to review and derive a consensus of market opinion early the following week.

**Bullish
Consensus
Percentage**

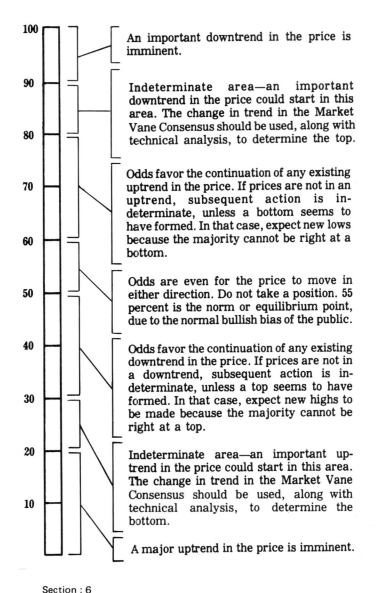

An important downtrend in the price is imminent.

Indeterminate area—an important downtrend in the price could start in this area. The change in trend in the Market Vane Consensus should be used, along with technical analysis, to determine the top.

Odds favor the continuation of any existing uptrend in the price. If prices are not in an uptrend, subsequent action is indeterminate, unless a bottom seems to have formed. In that case, expect new lows because the majority cannot be right at a bottom.

Odds are even for the price to move in either direction. Do not take a position. 55 percent is the norm or equilibrium point, due to the normal bullish bias of the public.

Odds favor the continuation of any existing downtrend in the price. If prices are not in a downtrend, subsequent action is indeterminate, unless a top seems to have formed. In that case, expect new highs to be made because the majority cannot be right at a top.

Indeterminate area—an important uptrend in the price could start in this area. The change in trend in the Market Vane Consensus should be used, along with technical analysis, to determine the bottom.

A major uptrend in the price is imminent.

Section : 6

FIGURE 1
Bullish consensus percentage.

118

It is useful to express the consensus of market opinions of those surveyed, after appropriate weighting, as a bullish percentage ranging from 0 to 100%. For example a bullish-consensus of 70% indicates that 70% of all the traders in a given commodity market such as cattle are bullishly inclined and think prices will move higher.

Research has revealed that 90% is too close to unanimity and, whenever a commodity achieves 90% bullishness, it is ripe for a downward reaction. Conversely, whenever a commodity is only 20% bullish (80% bearish), it is ripe for a rally. The imbalance in the percentages is due to the normal bullish bias of the typical trader. The norm or equilibrium point is 55%, and hence 20% and 90% are equivalent deviations from the norm.

The accompanying bullish consensus thermometer (Figure 1) illustrates the various market situations.

How to Use the Bullish Consensus

There are three basic ways to use the bullish consensus percentages:

1. Taking contrarian positions when the bullish consensus reaches extremes.
2. Trading with the trend of the bullish consensus.
3. An alert that a change in the present price trend is imminent.

Taking Contrarian Positions

As mentioned, the term "contrarian position" identifies those purchases or sales made at bullish extremes, that is, when the bullish consensus of speculators in the market is greater than 90% or less than 20%. In brief, it means taking a position that is contrary to practically everyone else in the market.

Here's an example of principle of contrary opinion in action. Assume a condition in which the bullish percentage for a particular commodity futures is 92%. This means that essentially all the speculators are bullish and are, therefore, anticipating a rise in the price. Because almost everyone is of the same opinion and has already bought, there are not enough speculators left to buy new positions and make the price move higher. As a result, there is only one way the prices can move— down! Confirmation that this condition exists occurs when the release of bullish news fails to move the prices higher. Bearish news, however, will cause a chain reaction through voluntary and involuntary exit of the longs from the market—the result is usually a catastrophic drop in the price. This is why there is almost always a large profit potential associated with contrarian trades.

In the above example the conditions could have been reversed and would have been equally applicable, that is, a bullish consensus of less than 20% which is the equivalent of 80% of the speculators being bearish. In this case a sharp rise in the price is almost certain to occur on the first bullish news.

Here are the principal rules for contrarian trading:

1. A contrarian position can usually be taken immediately when a bullish extreme is reached, greater than 90% or less than 20%. With caution, a contrarian position or an appropriate market order (e.g., an order to buy or sell on stop) can be placed any time the bullish consensus exceeds 80% or is less than 30%.

2. Watching the trend of the bullish percentages will alert you beforehand that bullish extremes are probably going to occur. When 80% or 30% is reached (the respective borders of the overbought and oversold areas), a sudden reversal in the price trend could occur at any time. The closer the bullish consensus approaches an extreme (100% or 0%), the greater the contrarian price move.

3. Open interest should be in the excess of 8000 contracts to ensure a reliable contrarian position. The larger the open interest, the more certain a contrarian position will be profitable.

4. *If the number of open contracts is increasing steadily, do not take a contrarian position, regardless of the bullish consensus.* The consensus is likely to remain high until the number of contracts stabilizes. The price trend is also likely to continue as long as the open interest is increasing—new speculators entering the market.

5. Make sure the market is principally speculators, not hedgers. Hedgers should hold fewer than 50% of the open contracts. The percentage of contracts held by hedgers can be found in the

CFTC REPORT 073177			CFTC REPORT 083177		
Trader	% Long	% Short	Trader	% Long	% Short
Large			Large		
Spec	02.6	05.3	Spec	00.9	07.5
Sprd	32.1	32.3	Sprd	33.6	33.9
Hedg	40.3	32.2	Hedg	39.8	23.1
Total	75.0	69.8	Total	74.3	64.5
Small	25.8	30.2	Small	25.7	35.5

FIGURE 2
Hedgers data from a typical
commitment report—soybeans.

Commitment of Traders report issued each month by the Commodity Futures Trading Commission. Data from a typical report are shown in Figure 2. Hedgers influence the prices mainly during the harvest period. Do not go opposite a crowd of hedgers.

6. Because the price volatility at tops and bottoms is typically higher than normal, close protective stops are not advisable when a contrarian position is first initiated. This will avoid whiplash losses. Bring the stop in closer to the current price once the contrarian move has started.

7. When a news event favorable to the consensus fails to move the price, it is a strong confirmation that a profitable contrarian position exists. Take a position quickly at this juncture, because the first contrary news event will probably result in a large price move favoring your contrary position.

Figures 3 through 6 illustrate typical contrarian situations indicated by bullish consensus extremes and the subsequent large price moves.

Bullish Consensus Trend Trading

The principle of bullish consensus trend trading is to trade with the consensus trend until a bullish extreme is reached.

Here are the general rules:

1. When changes in the absolute values of the bullish consensus in any one to two week period are:

5% or less—of questionable significance

5% to 10%—probably reflects a change in trader's attitude

10% or more—definitely reflects a change in trader's attitude

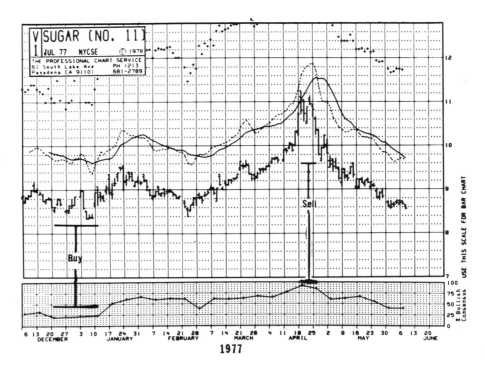

FIGURE 3
Typical contrarian situations—sugar, 1977.

FIGURE 4
Typical contrarian situation—wheat, 1978.

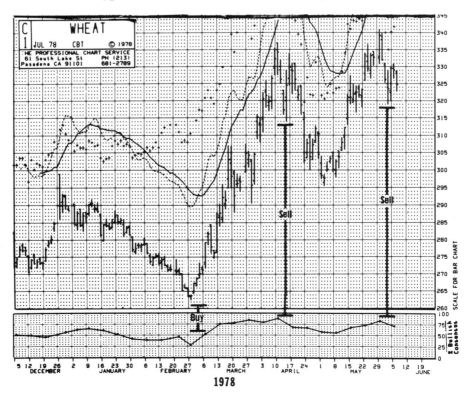

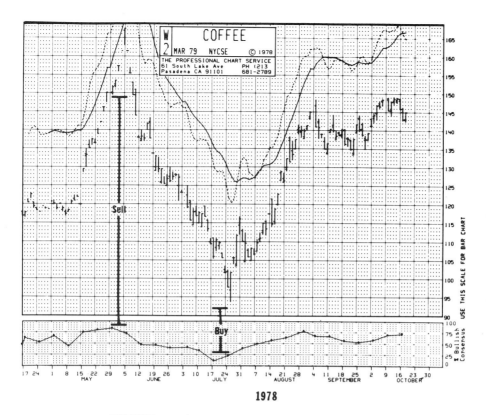

FIGURE 5
Typical contrarian situation—coffee, 1978.

FIGURE 6
Typical contrarian situation—cotton, 1977.

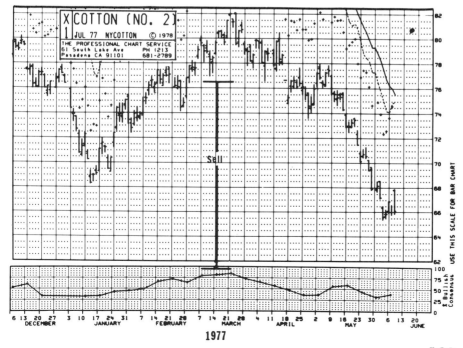

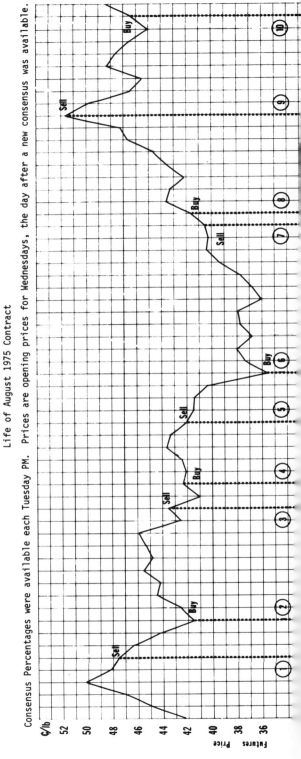

CATTLE

Life of August 1975 Contract

Consensus Percentages were available each Tuesday PM. Prices are opening prices for Wednesdays, the day after a new consensus was available.

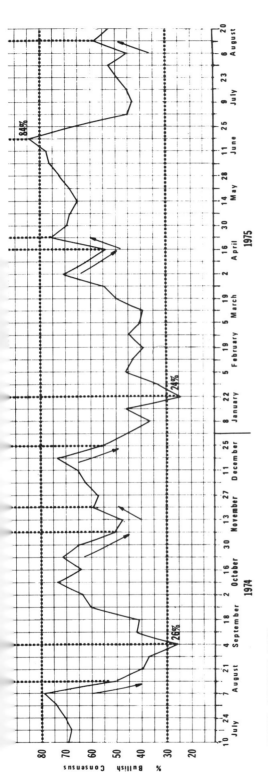

GENERAL CONSENSUS RULES:

●An overbought or an oversold condition begins to occur when the consensus exceeds 80% or is less than 30% respectively, and the Open Interest is either stable (changing less than 3% per week) or is decreasing.

●When the consensus is in the 60 to 80% area and a large decrease in the consensus occurs (approximately 10% or more in 1 to 2 weeks maximum), a significant drop in the prices is also likely to occur. The reverse is true in the 30 to 50% area.

COMMENTS:

② ⑥ Oversold condition exists - Buy ⎫ Note that one could have waited a week to confirm that the low (or high) in the consensus
⑨   Overbought condition exists - Sell ⎬ had occurred before taking a position and still caught the major part of the price move.
① ③ ⑤ ⑦ Sharp decrease in the consensus - Sell.   was a **false** signal which would have been evident the following
④ ⑧ ⑩ Sharp increase in the consensus - Buy.   week when both the prices and the Bullish Consensus rose.

FIGURE 7
Consensus trend as guide to trading.

125

2. A *long* position is optimally initiated in the 30 to 50% range following an absolute increase in the value of the bullish consensus of 10% or more in the prior week or prior two weeks.

3. A *short* position is optimally initiated in the 80 to 60% range following an absolute decrease in the value of the bullish consensus of 10% or more in the prior week or prior two weeks.

There have been periods of several months duration in various commodities such as cattle where the commodity could be very profitably traded using only the consensus trend; such a period is shown in Figure 7. Likewise there have been periods when this technique used only by itself would have produced large losses. The reasons for the variable capability is not understood and more research is required. It is suspected that this technique works best when the open interest is relatively stable. However, the unreliability of this technique does not invalidate its use as a secondary tool to confirm projected price trends derived from other market indicators. *In any event, the bullish consensus trend-following technique is not recommended as an exclusive indicator.*

Areas Deserving Special Comments

The following areas deserve special comments and are discussed in subsequent paragraphs:

Orderly/disorderly markets

Open interest

Timing

News events

Bullish consensus accuracy and range

Commodity applicability

Market composition—large speculators, hedgers, and small speculators

Required data

When contrarian positions don't work

Orderly/Disorderly Market

When a particular market such as soybeans becomes disorderly, that is, repeated limit moves and the like, many market analysts recommend moving to the sidelines, a neutral position rated as 55%. Consequently, in periods during which a disorderly market occurs, it is very difficult to obtain meaningful bullish consensus figures on that particular commodity. Hence bullish consensus percentages should not be used as the basis for action during such periods.

Open Interest

Rising open interest indicates that new speculators are entering the market and/or old speculators are taking additional positions. A rapid change in open interest, for example, a change of about 3% in one week, indicates that the market is in a state of flux; consequently, the consensus figures are not likely to reflect the true picture. *Note that it is essential to monitor the open interest for the principal individual contract rather than simply the total open interest for all contracts.* Immediately prior to the expiration of the nearby contract, the total open interest figures can be very misleading. See Figure 8 which depicts the open interest for the individual contract month and the total for all contracts. A key point—*the bullish consensus figures can remain at extremes as long as the open interest continues to increase.* Pertinent points related to open interest can be summarized as follows:

1. If the open interest is increasing steadily, do not take a contrarian position, regardless of the bullish consensus. The consensus is likely to remain high until the number of contracts stabilizes. Prices are also likely to continue their present trend as long as open interest is increasing.

2. Open Interest should be in excess of 8000 contracts to ensure a reliable contrarian position. The larger the open interest, the more certain a contrarian position will be profitable.

3. The larger the open interest, the lower the risk in taking a contrarian position.

4. If the open interest is decreasing rapidly, for example, in excess of 3% per week, only a small contrarian price move is likely.

Timing

The criticalness of timing in taking a contrarian position increases as a bullish consensus extreme is approached as long as the open interest is

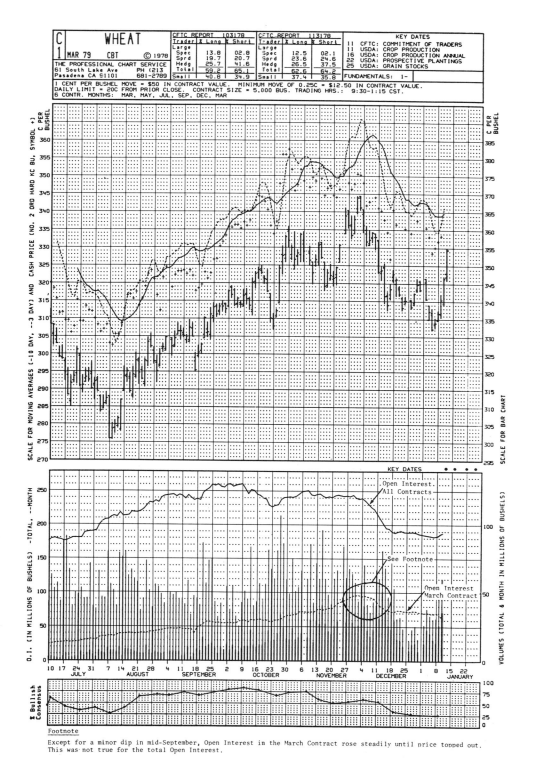

FIGURE 8
Monthly open interest data.

Footnote

Except for a minor dip in mid-September, Open Interest in the March Contract rose steadily until price topped out. This was not true for the total Open Interest.

not rising rapidly—as covered in detail in another section of this article. For example, when the bullish consensus for cocoa on February 22, 1978 was 8%, you take a long position immediately—the following day prices began to rally, and in the next five weeks they rose over 45¢ in the July contract, an increase in value of $13,500 per contract. Generally when the overbought and oversold borders are reached, 80% and 30%, respectively, it is advisable to wait and see if the bullish consensus trend reverses the following week. Normally, one to two weeks are required for a contrarian move to develop after the 30% and 80% are touched. Once a contrarian position has been established, the bullish consensus is of little value as an exit indicator. However, if you are trading with the majority, bullish consensus trend trading, the consensus figures are an excellent tool to help you exit from the market just prior to a major reversal.

News Events

When a news event corresponding to the consensus (i.e., a bullish news event when the bullish consensus is above 80%,) fails to move prices higher, it is a strong confirmation that a profitable contrarian position exists. A situation such as this indicates that the majority of bullishly inclined traders have already taken their long positions and there are insufficient bulls left to drive prices higher by their buying. The reverse situation is equally true.

Market Composition—
Hedgers, Large and Smaller Speculators

Market hedgers, by virtue of their position in the cash commodity market, essentially remove themselves from both the cash and future markets, by neutralizing their cash positions using futures. Consequently they do not react to price fluctuations in the futures market like a speculator would. Therefore, contrarian trading works best when the market is principally speculators—not hedgers. Refer to the Commitment of Traders published each month by the Commodity Future Trading Commission for a breakdown of the type of traders in a given commodity market—Figure 2 is a tabulation of the data in a typical report. Hedgers influence the prices mainly during the harvest periods. Do not go opposite to a crowd of hedgers. For example, if the Bullish Consensus is 88% in a particular commodity, a short contrarian position should be considered. However, if 60% of the long contracts were held by hedgers who represent very strong hands financially, the down-side contrarian move is likely to be very small or not occur at all. *In short, the ideal contrarian position is one opposite to a large number of small traders and a minimum number of hedgers and large speculators.* Restated, a good contrarian position is likely to be shared by a majority of the hedgers and large speculators and a minority of small traders. In most commodities the preponderance of hedging is on the short side by the producer—not the long side by the processor, who can usually pass along any cost increases to the consumer. Since a good contrarian trade is normally shared by the majority of the hedgers, the best contrarian trades in markets having a significant number of hedgers are more likely to be on the short side rather than the long side.

Bullish Consensus Accuracy and Ranges

Knowing that the bullish consensus is derived from the opinions of analysts provides an insight. Practically all analysts have an opinion on the principal commodities such as wheat, beans, cattle, and silver. Consequently, the bullish consensus for these commodities represents a large sampling and hence has a greater probability of being accurate. Likewise, the percentage figures are less likely to reach extremes. On the other hand, *for thinly traded commodities such as broilers and eggs, the week-to-week fluctuations in the bullish consensus are likely to be greater, less accurate, and reach extremes more often.* This is easily seen by taking the hypothetical commodity "red herring" which is covered by only one analyst—the bullish consensus figures could be 0% or 100%, or for that matter anything in between. There is also the possibility that he might be on vacation one week and no figure at all would be available.

In summary, experience has revealed when the bullish consensus for the principal commodities exceeds 85% or is less than 25%, an exceptional opportunity usually exists.

Commodity Applicability

Bullish consensus data has been compiled weekly since March 1964, and with the exception of a few missing weeks, the data by year are available to researchers and analysts.

Commodities covered for the years traded include:

Oats	Bellies	Potatoes	Copper	GNMA
Corn	Hogs	Orange Juice	Platinum	T-bills
Wheat	Cattle	Sugar	Silver	
Beans	Broilers	Cocoa	Gold	
Oil	Eggs	Coffee		
Meal				

Insufficient time has passed to fully evaluate the applicability of the bullish consensus to GNMAs and T-bills.

For all commodities other than GNMAs and T-bills, contrary opinion has repeatedly demonstrated year after year its capability to identify major market turns.

Required Data

To use contrary opinion for predicting futures market action, the following data and information are needed:

1. Bullish consensus (weekly).
2. Open interest by principal contracts (daily)—the total open interest for all contracts can be misleading, particularly just prior to the expiration of the nearby contract.
3. Committment of Traders report (monthly)—issued on the 11th of each month by the Commodity Futures Trading Commission.
4. News (daily).
5. Prices: open, high, low and close (daily)—preferably plotted as a bar chart.

When Contrarian Positions Don't Work

A restatement and an analysis of the definition of a contrarian position is appropriate here:

A contrarian position exists when the majority of the traders in a specific commodity have committed their allocated funds to the same position, either long or short.

Based on the above definition, here are the factors that can influence the effectiveness of a contrarian position:

1. Was the sampling of analysts large enough and their opinions appropriately weighted to produce an accurate bullish consensus?

2. Are speculators following the advice of the advisors?

3. Analysts views are subject to change and there is a delay of several days between acquisition of the information and tabulation of the consensus.

4. News events can bring new people into the market and/or cause old speculators to dig deeper into their pocketbooks to finance new positions. Open interest data, which reveals this situation, are not available from most markets until the next day.

5. Has the makeup of the market (i.e., hedgers, large speculator, and small speculator), changed since compiling the last bullish-consensus?

All the above factors are so-called "gray areas" rather than being black or white and therefore only influence the bullish consensus in terms of degree. In general, the bullish consensus almost invariably calls the market turns within a matter of a week or two weeks—the greatest area of difficulty is selecting an appropriate price and time to enter the market and thereby minimize your risk.

Gary Ginter *brings a knowledge of philosophy, sociology, economics, statistics, and computer science to his study of the commodity markets. A Phi Beta Kappa graduate of USC, his unusually diverse background also includes the position of director of research for Precious Metals, Inc., and independent research in the fields of combustion technology and pollution control. In 1974 he founded, along with Joseph Ritchie, a specialized firm, Chicago Research and Trading, which trades exclusively for its own account in all commodities.*

Joe Ritchie's *trading career includes serving as head trader for Precious Metals, Inc., for whom he ran a cash bullion and gold coin trading room. Prior to founding Chicago Research and Trading, Joe was president of a clearing member of the Chicago Board of Trade, A-Mark Trading Corporation, which specialized in silver futures arbitrage between New York and Chicago. Chicago Research and Trading specializes in gold and silver arbitrage and floor trading of the soybean crush. Joe holds a B.A. from Wheaton College in philosophy, and attributes his business acumen to the fact that he never took any business or economics courses.*

The foundation of technical analysis, as well as all of commodity trading, is the market price. The development of systems is usually based on observing price patterns and formulating rules of varying complexity to profit from these patterns. As the interest in commodities increases rapidly, there are a greater number of analysts who have never experienced a familiarity with the actual trading process which occurs on the exchange; instead, they have studied daily price quotations from the newspapers or used historical data tapes provided by one of the supporting computer companies.

While some analysts get as close to the market as a display screen, and watch the individual price movements during the day, their limited exposure to actual trading leaves an important gap in the process of creating a trading method that will operate effectively. In the following article Gary Ginter and Joseph Ritchie discuss the problems of price data which are transparent to the analyst who is removed from the trading floor. They consider the successive fills as a price continuum which often has gaps based on the momentary change of volume. This variation in liquidity throughout the day is only one important problem that is generally overlooked by the technician. Other areas of concern are the selection of the appropriate order, the execution cost (the cost of doing business) and how to minimize the problems.

As technical analysis becomes more popular it will be more competitive. Some operators will be successful by using more sophisticated, faster-feedback equipment which will give them instantaneous information as the trades occur. Others will rely on slower methods using less electronics; those analysts will need a more complete and realistic understanding of the market process such as the experience of Gary Ginter and Joseph Ritchie can provide. This presentation has been edited from the "Technical Analysis in Commodities Symposium," held on October 18, 1978, at the Hotel Pierre in New York.

DATA ERRORS AND PROFIT DISTORTIONS

GARY GINTER

JOSEPH J. RITCHIE

There is an expression in computer lingo: "GIGO: garbage in, garbage out." With the mixed blessing of the coming of computers into our field, perhaps the more appropriate phrase would be "GILO: garbage in, losses out." Putting bad data into the computer may result in having more than just "garbage" out; there may be losses, and red ink. Bad data is "garbage," and a very bad sort of "garbage" to be sure.

A technician faces data problems of many types. They can be divided into two main groups: (1) the problems inherent in the data itself, that is, inaccurate data; and (2) the problems inherent in the way the data is used, that is, misapplied data (which may or may not be accurate).

Inaccurate Data Problems

As for the first, problems inherent in the data per se, problems of inaccuracy are primarily a function of liquidity. As all who have traded the market know, liquidity is more a function of time than anything else (outside perhaps of the commodity itself). The farther out one goes in selecting a delivery month in which to trade, the less liquid it is; the wider the spread one faces between the bid and ask because of the lack of liquidity, and therefore the more the cost of executing a trade. When paying commissions, it may be cheaper to buy forward deliveries if you intend to hold a position, rather than churning your account. But for those of us on the floor, this execution cost of doing business is the primary cost consideration.

Different commodities have different degrees of liquidity. For example, soybeans are much more liquid than broilers. If you don't think so, trade them.

Another type of liquidity also exists. A very good example would be in the soybean crush where Joe Ritchie and I have the most experience. It is the new crop/old crop phenomenon. There can be very good liquidity in July and November and extremely poor liquidity in September, so much so that you should never try to trade September based on charts. Prices are quite unrealistic, which can be seen when the September/November spread shows considerably more volatility when compared to July/November. Many people are familiar with these types of problems. The same thing would apply to metal switches such as Board of Trade or IMM silver or gold, compared to, say, Comex switches. Because of their call (their switch call after the close), Comex switches are kept very well in line and very dependable. In comparing the one year carry, Comex December/December for example, to the Board of Trade December/December, it can be seen that the price variation between the two comparable spreads over the year will be due to the lack of a closing call on the Board of Trade.

So there are liquidity problems, there are institutional factors like the lack of a call on the Board of Trade or the IMM, and then there are limit problems.

Limit Problems

I think the best, at least the most relevant to us, was the old crush limit problem which existed before the limits were expanded for soybeans. You had a larger relative limit in oil and meal combined, compared to the maximum soybean move in a day, so that a day which was limit up or limit down gave you a big margin problem or else a really big margin windfall. Since last year the crush, as you know, is more in line because the bean limits were expanded to 30¢, which is more appropriate given the limits on meal and oil.

Limit problems can be a pitfall, especially with a complex spread relationship such as the cattle feeding margin. The extremely wide point swings in that spread may be more a function of a limit move that day in some related commodity rather than in an actual tradeable value that was in the pits and executable either in or out. So watch out for limit problems.

Misuse of Data

Those examples should adequately cover the two primary types of inherent problems in data: liquidity and institutional problems. Next, there is the problem of misusing the data. Good data, fed into the historical test of a trading system that you are evaluating, can still result in misleading information with respect to profits and losses. There are a few reasons why this happens.

Figure 1 represents what we call the daily price/volume distribution. In the figure:

aa' represents the assumption of volume homogeneity.

bb' represents the assumption that volume is some decreasing function as you move away from the center of the trading range.

cc' represents the per lot profit contribution of a fading system . . . [on a day when bb' approximates the actual price-volume distribution of trades].

dd' represents the approximate total profit contribution of all trades made at any given price in a fading system . . . [on a day when bb' approximates the actual price-volume distribution of trades].

L represents the low price.

H represents the high price.

M represents the mid-point.

This diagram is intended to show that any trading range is composed of a volume/price distribution of intraday prices. It can be seen that the volume—the liquidity of trading—tends to be bunched towards the center of the range. Of course, there are a lot of obvious exceptions, like orange juice—I have been trying to buy it for four days and if you have watched the market, you know the problem. (Every trade that has occurred has been locked at the top of the limit). But for most days, Figure 1 will hold true. One of the basic sources of misleading data for technicians is the assumption represented by the straight line;

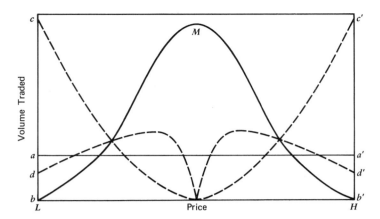

FIGURE 1
Daily price/volume distribution.

namely that the distribution function of trades is a homogeneous one, that it is even across all ranges over the entire day. Any trader knows that is not true at all. In fact, there may only have been one trade at the day's high or low; and if there were stop-orders near it, there probably was only one trade.

The dotted line represents the apparent profit for a technical system that makes the assumption of a straight line volume distribution. If the system is "fading" the market, the results come out at a value some place around the mean. For the results to be near the mean, it is obvious that the contribution of the trades closest to the middle will be relatively small and the contribution of the trades most extreme will be large. If you assume that you can get one price as easily as another; as the straight line distribution assumes, you will quickly find out that what seems to be very profitable on paper will, in fact, be not so profitable in use. Therefore, inflated profits can result from misapplying data on the basis of the distribution of data with respect to price/volume.

Stop-order and Limit-order Problems

There is an additional problem of where to place stop-orders and how stops tend to affect the market. Many traders are well aware of the problems and do not place stops in the market, but others still do, and these stops and limit orders tend to affect the market even before the prices get there. You can talk about this phenomenon as a gravitational model, where the amount of effect is inversely proportional to the distance between your stop and the current market price; therefore, if a stop is placed below the market at 48 and the market only traded to 50 in terms of the incoming orders, someone might try to push the price down to reach 48. The trader who has had the stop order filled at 48 gets the worst of both worlds with respect to the price/volume distribution; the market stops get filled when touched, whereas an action signal generated by a trading system, namely, a buy or sell signal, cannot depend on getting its executions at the desired prices. If you are only trading one lot this problem may not exist, but it does exist for larger positions; even one lot will cost some small amount to execute. In summary, the type of distribution shown in Figure 1 means that you compound two execution problems: you get the worst possible fills on your stop orders and not as good a fill as it would have appeared on your theoretical entries (your limit orders).

Execution Cost

The other major factor in creating realistic profit/loss tests based on historical data series analysis is the execution cost. If one wants to move a position when an action signal occurs, for example, a buy at 50, not all executions will be at 50; they will be at 50 plus delta, where delta is the cost of entering that position. This cost is not commissions, but the results of trading some quantity of contracts at a specific price; you cannot do an infinite amount of trading at any one price.

This execution cost (C) is a function which varies directly with quantity (Q) of contracts being traded in response to your action signals, as well as the volatility (V) of the commodity. The cost varies inversely with the liquidity of the commodity (L_c) times the liquidity of the option being traded (L_o). That is,

$$C = K \frac{Q \times V}{L_c \times L_o}$$

where:

C = Execution cost
Q = quantity of contracts being bought or sold
V = volatility of the commodity being traded
L_c = Liquidity of commodity being traded
L_o = Liquidity of option being traded
K = a constant

Now, if we define the following terms:

H = Highest price of the day in the option being traded
L = Lowest price of the day in that option
V_c = Total volume of contracts traded in all delivery options of the commodity that day
V_o = Volume of contracts traded that day in the delivery month you are trading

then:

$$Q = \sqrt[1.7]{Q}$$

$$V = \frac{2(H-L)}{H+L}$$

$$L_c = \sqrt{V_c}$$

$$L_o = \sqrt[2.5]{\frac{V_o}{V_c}}$$

and therefore:

$$C = K \frac{\sqrt[1.7]{Q}\left(\frac{2(H-L)}{H+L}\right)}{\sqrt{V_c}\sqrt[2.5]{\frac{V_o}{V_c}}}$$

This represents the execution cost portion of the total cost of making a trade. The other portion of your variable cost is the commission you pay, which would be added to the cost of execution. Remember, of course, that this is only the execution *cost*, and the average *price* at which you would move the position will be the midpoint of the range in which you are working—the closing range, for example, plus or minus this cost. If you are buying, the result will be the midpoint plus the cost. If you are selling, the price would be the midpoint minus the cost.

These are the factors that Joe's pit experience has taught us, and this equation is his first approximation of execution cost based on that experience.

We have discussed some of the data problems and included some of the ways that you might include the effect of execution costs in historical profit and loss testing. We can now consider other ways to minimize the problem of the data per se.

Accurate Data Sources

In doing complex spread relationships, we have found that one of the best data sources available to us for the Board of Trade is the CBT pulpit price log books. There is a person in each pit who records price sequences, mostly for the purpose of arbitration. There is no recording of volume, only price sequence. For example, a sequence might read 9:01 December meal (price), 9:01½ December meal (price), and so on. These sequences are written continuously all day. The result allows you to make an "eyeball" estimate of how much was traded at a given price. It is very much an intuitive judgment, but as of now it is one that is much better than anything else available. It would help if these log books were computerized. In a sense, they are indirectly available, because Comtrend and similar services have the exchange data base on line. You can use some of the computerized data for an analysis of these complex spreads by limiting its use to their shorter time spans. If you use more than a 6-day time span you may get inaccurate prices. To save some time when you are looking at the crush, display the spread on the 60-day plot and check all your extreme points with the one day spread chart, to see if the one day crush chart still retains those points. If it doesn't, then those points never really occurred in the pits.

Computer Pitfalls

It should be noted that the computer, although holding great promise, also holds the potential of doing our industry a disservice. By the very fact that this data and analysis come out of the computer-correlations and so on—there is an aura of credibility about what may be bad data. Perhaps more importantly, the convenience of the computer has made the running of statistical correlations (what we call shotgun correlations in sociology) seductively easy. Anyone can crank everything against everything else and have a high likelihood of coming out with a "successful" system which has no sound theory behind it and therefore no forecasting ability beyond pure coincidence. All good technical systems work for theoretically sound reasons reflecting human psychological tendencies. If you don't know why it works, you won't be able to tell when it would likely not work due to changed conditions.

On Maintaining Perspective

Whether or not you have a data problem depends on the length of time you expect to hold a position. If you are a floor trader trying to make one-half cent per bushel scalping or spreading, then data problems can have a critical effect on your historical profit or loss testing of floor trading models. But if you are a speculator trying to catch a one dollar move in the price of beans, then you cannot be hurt too badly by data problems. Fortunately, off-floor, non-member traders usually have such high commission costs that they can only afford to take longer term positions. It is probably not much consolation, but high commission costs minimize the relevance of data problems!

Have a feel for how the data problems relate to running historical tests for hypothetical profits and losses. Do not confuse what is basically an illusory execution profit (that is, profits on paper which will be lost in actual execution) for a real system profit. You will only be fooling yourself unless you can execute as well as a floor trader. You may make money anyway if you have a sound system, but you must recognize the existence of these data problems and treat them separately in order to know what you are doing that is making you money.

If you are going to be a floor trader, you must consider everything as a type of arbitrage, and this arbitrage is related to the idea of how far above or below the mean prices should go and what this mean was 10 seconds ago. You will always trade as if prices will return to the mean. You will occasionally lose, but in the long run you're going to come out profitably.

The speculator also arbitrages in a sense. He "fades" the world just as the floor trader "fades" the market orders that come into the pit. The speculator is saying "The whole world's wrong. I know that the price should be higher than it is—so I'll buy it." The speculator hopes to be arbitraging between what the price is and what it "should be." He may be right, but the speculator is in the same situation as the admiring mother who looked at her little Johnny, the only child out of step in the parade, and said, "Johnny's the only one in step!" Johnny may be the only one in step. But, as Shakespeare put it, "The truth will out.' And, of course, it always does. But the speculator's problem is two-fold: first, when the truth finally does out, was he in step or out? And secondly, while waiting for the truth to become apparent, will he run out of margin money? Speaking from personal experience, I can assure you that the latter case is far more frustrating than the former. To have been closed out of a position at a loss when if you could have just held on a bit longer . . . ah, but it's all a matter of "timing"— or so we are told by self-proclaimed commodity experts. And indeed it is. After all, even being in step is just a matter of timing!

Computer testing of a trading hypothesis can generate a mountain of data. Wringing out a moving average with 20 different time spans and 20 possible stop-loss "distances," for example, creates a minimum of 400 numbers. Introducing a third variable with 20 possible values would increase total data to 8000 numbers. Correlating them as handfuls of print-out would be virtually impossible.

Mapping is a technique that relates the test data spatially, much as an Army topographical map relates ground elevations to make peaks, valleys, and plateaus easily recognizable.

In the following discussion Mr. Kaufman shows you how to go about mapping the results of a commodity market test strategy and how the map may be interpreted. He also discusses the effects of slow versus fast moving averages, how a plateau of "poor" performance can be used to advantage by speculators, the benefits and shortcomings of "smoothing" data, dynamic versus static testing, and application of the principles to point-and-figure charts.

THE MAPPING SYSTEM OF TEST STRATEGY

PERRY J. KAUFMAN

The mapping system is a generalized testing procedure that presents the results of a trading model in terms of variations in two parameters. It gives the user a means for evaluating the performance of a trading method over a range of specific measurement criteria. For example, an analyst may be interested in the results of using a simple moving average. Instead of testing a 20-day moving average, the mapping system will test a range of moving averages using incremental steps. By specifying moving averages from 2 through 40 in steps of 2, we will get the results of using 2, 4, 6, . . . , 38 and 40 day moving averages. The results will show the areas of success based on historic testing, and with proper investigation and use the results may have predictive qualities.

But the map is not one-dimensional, and our example only varies the speed or length of the moving average. It is also reasonable to test the use of a stop-loss which may be a function of price level, expressed in percent. The trading model expects higher prices to result in greater volatility and therefore greater risk.

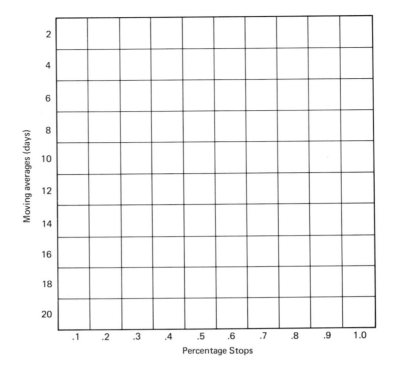

FIGURE 1
The mapping system of test strategy.

The simplest calculation for adjusting to this phenomena is to use a percentage of either the current price or the moving average applied as a stop-loss. We can then test incremental values of both the moving average and the stop-loss as shown in Figure 1.

In this example it is important to see the continuity of the two parameters being tested. A faster moving average is more sensitive to price change and should expect better results using a closer stop-loss. As the moving average slows, it seems reasonable to move the stop-loss further away. For that reason Figure 1 shows the direction of the scaling indices in such a way that the upper left corner represents the fastest moving average and the closest stops; the lower right corner has the slowest moving average with the farthest stops. There is continuity in all directions. Represented as a map, we can see that the continuity of the results of many tests can be most easily observed. Not only can the single best set of variables be isolated, but the depth of success based on incremental variation can be easily seen.

Interpreting the Results

For most systems the displayed results will show continuous areas of successful results similar to a contour map. There will be an area of intense success surrounded by bands of declining success. Very often there are two unique sections of the map that will show good performance: one in the slow sector and one in the fast. By slow we mean infrequent trading (one to five per year) and by fast we mean frequent (20 or more). This will occur more often in the very volatile commodities where the higher prices cause a stratification of the speed of a technique. Extreme price fluctuations will permit profits when trading the very short term, erratic movements, or it will allow the trader to stand far back of these movements and trade the major trend. Figure 2 shows the application of a moving average with a specified stop-loss to both high and low price levels and its related test maps. In part *a* we see that prices fluctuate in a narrower range at low levels, permitting a medium-speed moving average to perform successfully over the tested data. Only one group of profitable results will normally show on the map, as represented in part *b* of Figure 2. The slight variation of the solid moving average line in the price chart will capture more or fewer

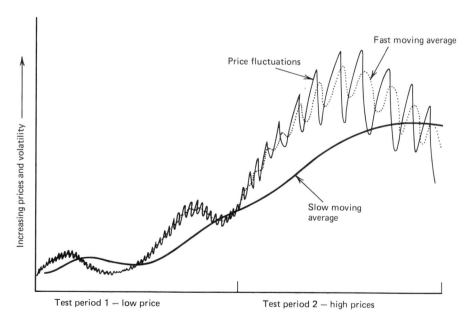

FIGURE 2a
Price movement.

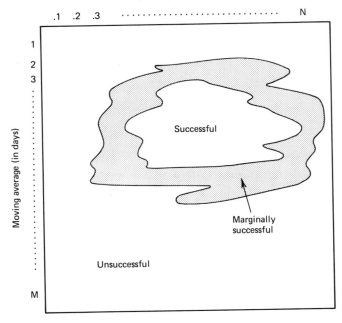

FIGURE 2b
Test map results for
Period 1—low prices.

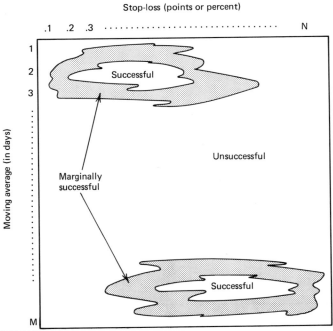

FIGURE 2c
Test map results for
Period 2—high price.

profits until it becomes too fast and has many frequent losses or too slow and fails to take any profits. There is not enough fluctuation in the small daily price moves to permit the successful trading of a very fast moving average at low price levels (test period 1).

As prices move higher we see in test period 2 that fluctuations become disproportionately larger. There is now enough latitude in the price variation itself to successfully apply a fast moving average. The medium-speed average used at the lower levels to identify the trend will no longer work, since it will be frequently violated by the severe fluctuations of the short-term price movement. To successfully identify the trend of prices at higher levels it is necessary to apply a slower moving average. Figure 2, part c shows the nature of the results using a test map during period 2. In the upper left and lower right sections of the map we find smaller areas of successful combinations of moving averages and stop-loss criteria. Neither area has any common overlapping of the selected area in part b. The upper left part of the map represents a fast moving average with a close stop-loss, and the lower right shows the results of a slow average with a distance stop-loss criteria.

Transitionary Steps

If we were to run sequential tests on a commodity that moved from low to high levels as shown in Figure 2a, we would be able to observe a unique movement of the contour of success. As prices moved higher and began to fluctuate more widely, we would see the area of successful performance broaden, permitting a wider range of moving averages and stop-loss selections. But as prices continued higher, this larger area would split into two areas somewhere near to the center of its formation. The successful areas near the middle would immediately contract, leaving the outside portions (top and bottom) to define the direction of successful moving averages to be used. This situation is quite analogous to the splitting of an amoeba.

An interesting characteristic of the test map is its relationship to a moving test period. If we were to perform retesting of the price chart (part a) at regular intervals using all data from the beginning of the chart, we would bias our results toward slower moving averages. During the very low priced intervals the faster trading systems would be generating losses, while the slow averages may do very little or show small, unrealized profits in the direction of the long-term trend. When we build up to the final interval we then offset the recent success of the faster trading criteria with earlier losses while we may augment the slower performers with prior profits. The final results will show that the slower trading methods, those that operated on the longer term trend, had the most successful performance.

This same conclusion will apply to tests over test periods of many years taken as a combination of shorter time intervals. When looking for a single set of variables for a trading method that would have performed successfully during the past 10 years, the most uniform results will be in the slower parameters. Although it may be that the faster methods netted to most profits in years with extreme price movements, they often alternated periods of profits and losses with the net result being a loss.

Recording and Averaging Performance

Up to now we have discussed performance in general terms, referring only to the relative success of selected combinations of variables. Since each box or juncture of the test map represents a unique computer test run (simulation), it can contain more than one piece of information. For simplicity, we will consider saving the profit (in percent of margin), the number of trades performed during the test period, and the number of profitable trades taken as a percentage of total trades, called reliability. These three pieces of summary data will be enough to define a simple method for evaluating the test maps.

Assuming that only one piece of data was recorded, for example profits, we would be interested in smoothing the contours to determine best overall area of performance, rather than locating an isolated test of peak performance. We are now touching on considerations of predictability using this technique. We make the assumption here that the last performance during an historic period will be reasonably indicative of an area of good performance in the future. This topic will be discussed in more detail later. Rather than assume a pinpoint relationship between the past and the future, we chose to average a group of tests on the map and develop a smoothed contour.

The practical approach to smoothing is to take a set of nine tests forming a square, average all the test values, and put the average of those nine tests into a new map in the position of the center box. This operation would be performed for all sets of nine boxes; when we move along the outside edges of the map we use only six boxes and in the corners only four. In general, a nine-box average is shown in Figure 3. The number of boxes averaged should relate to the size of the test map; averaging an area that is too large may move the final selected area to a position between two or more good areas, but not to an area that had performed independently well. Once the averages have been accumulated in a new map, a selection of the best performance will be the same as selecting the best average area.

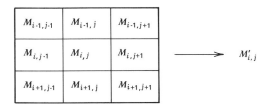

(a)   Center average (9 box)

(b)   Top edge average (6 box)

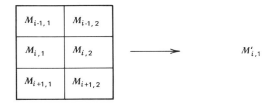

(c)   Left edge average (6 box)

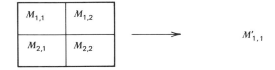

(d)   Upper left corner average (4 box)

FIGURE 3
Averaging of results.

Testing Strategy

Profits may not be the only criteria that is desired for determining the success of a system test. We can reason that a high profit which was the result of a single unusual sustained move, offsetting many losing trades, may not be a good indicator of future success. Even though we get spectacular price moves from time to time in varying commodities, it is not our plan to rely on these moves exclusively for our success.

The percentage of profitable to total trades, defined as *reliability*, will indicate the ability for a system to take profits with consistency. Reliability can be used to find those situations where profits were achieved through a single, unusual price move. Although a high reliability may seem desirable, it may also represent an extreme fine-tuning of the system being tested. If the low reliability represents one or two exceptional situations and the highest reliabilities show extremely critical decisions, we will be looking for the mid-ranges.

The number of total trades can be used as indication of the standard error, given as

$$E = \frac{1}{\sqrt{N}}$$

The error is 100% when there is only one trade, 71% for two trades, 25% for four trades, and so on. Each test result should be adjusted for this problem.

There are a few simple formulas that would operate on the three elements (profit, reliability, and number of trades) and combine their values into a single score which would be better than any one taken separately. We can start with profits and reduce the value by the other factors, resulting in a "relative" profit. Since the reliability is dependent on the number of trades, we will apply our standard error to the reliability

$$R' = R \cdot \left(1 - \frac{1}{\sqrt{N}} \right)$$

giving a value discounted by the error factor. If the reliability R was 60% on five trades, we get $.60 \times .55 = .33$, or a 33% reliability. (If R is not altered it will favor increasing reliability.) It can be seen that two trades of 100% reliability (both profitable) is only as significant as a large number of trades with 30% reliability ($R = 1.00, E = 1/\sqrt{2}$, then $R' = 29.3\%$). By multiplying the profits of each test by R' we can discount the effects of either a single large profit (low reliability) or only a few trades (poor sample). However, if the returns were so large that they were out of proportion with all other results, the discounted profits would still determine the best selection of variables to use.

Dynamic versus Static

Test strategy falls into the two primary categories of dynamic and static, representing philosophies of continuous or single testing procedures, respectively. Static testing is the simplest conceptually; it conforms to the principle that a single trading method using well-defined elements can be found to have worked in the past and continue to work in the future. The elements of the system can cause variations in its signal generation because of changes in price levels, patterns, or other technical phenomena, but the method and formulas are all fixed.

The dynamic test concept is one of either varying the speed or duration of the technique or of changing analytic techniques because of changes in market situations. These changes occur according to an orderly, predetermined set of rules.

Static Testing

The mapping system we have discussed can be used to determine the variables of a trading method that is intended to work under the continuously changing conditions of the commodities markets. A simple example using moving averages was used in our previous maps: testing of all combinations of the speed of a moving average versus a stop-loss criteria which is a percentage of the current price level or the current calculated moving average value. It is assumed that the varying stop-loss adjusts the risk as price levels change, allowing the system to stay with the trend regardless of the volatility.

Static testing would also permit multidimensional testing using the mapping system. The basic trending system described in the previous paragraph could be filtered with a timing device for entry and exit. If we define the timing formula to be a momentum index accompanied by an increase in sales volume, we can independently test the variations in short-term momentum along one axis of the map and the magnitude of the change in volume along the other axis. If tested independently, each showing success, it is likely that the combined method will be successful.

During the testing process each set of variables must be tested over sufficient time periods and generate enough trades to give significant results. A performance profile should be created to allow you to anticipate the number of profitable and losing trades as well as the probable size of a profit and loss. If some historic period is not used for developmental testing, it can then be used to test the final selected system. The performance during this trial test should be within the expected performance levels given by the original tests. Failure to perform as expected should imply that the system does not anticipate and adjust for variations in market conditions.

Dynamic Testing

Using dynamic testing, we take the approach that changes in market movement itself should cause changes in either the system being used or the variables of the system used. It is assumed that no amount of comprehensive testing or mathematical formulas can account for or predict the type of price fluctuation that the market will exhibit. The test strategy will be reapplied at well-defined intervals, and the results of the tests will cause new parameters or systems to be used until the next retesting occurs.

We can use the test map for moving averages as our example of dynamic testing. In our previous discussions of static testing we would apply the test map to find the best results using the speed of the moving average (in days) and a stop-loss criteria (in percent or points) as the two variables. But the most important part of the static test was that it was performed only once. The amount of data used for testing should be sufficiently long to provide significance. Although results could be composed of a combination of many shorter tests, the objective of testing was to find the best set of variables to use for trading the system.

If we use 10 unique tests of one calendar year each, take the best results of each year, and apply those parameters to the next year's trading, we have an extrapolative, dynamic test. Since performance is determined on a time interval following the test period, we have a simple predictive test situation due to extrapolation; the repetitive use of a short test interval to determine the parameters for the system makes this a dynamic method. We can see that the length of the interval used for testing and the length of the interval used for extrapolation, or trading, are the most important choices to be made by the analyst.

The Test and Trading Intervals

We have previously discussed the relationship of the test interval and the speed of the moving average that performs best; that concept still holds for dynamic testing. The selection of a shorter test interval will result in the best performance in the area of faster moving averages with closer stop-losses. More important is the length of interval over which the results can be used before retesting is necessary. Consider a test interval of 200 days, approximately 9 to 10 months. If we were to retest every day by dropping off the oldest day's data and adding the most recent, we would have introduced only $1/200$ or $1/2$ of one percent of new data. The results shown on the test map would probably be indistinguishable from the test of the prior day; the likelihood that the best parameters would change is small.

Now consider an extremely long trading period, equal to the original test period. After 200 days of applying the parameters which were selected from the prior test, we would be working with all new data. The next test map may have no relationship to the prior one since it shares no common data. The position of the best selection of parameters could be completely removed from the area of selection for the prior interval. This consideration leads us to think of the results in a way that coordinates the probable movement of the best parameters on the test map over a fixed period, using the area averaging technique discussed in *Recording and Averaging Performance*. We would like the parameters selected as best during this test to be in the most successful contour in the next test. This coordination can only be accomplished by observing individual tests of the system used; a 10% projection using a 200-day test and a nine-box average may be a good place to start (Figure 4).

The intention of the dynamic test is to keep the system parameters in the best area of the test map. As the market moves to higher prices and the test interval remains the same, there will be a shift to a faster moving average; when prices decline and become less volatile, the selected

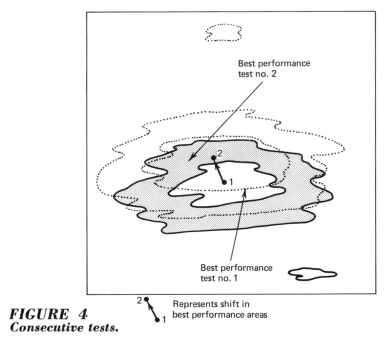

FIGURE 4
Consecutive tests.

2 • Represents shift in
1 • best performance areas

parameters will be near the bottom of the test map. It is most likely that in static testing only one moving average would have to be used for all situations.

Data To Be Tested

The data used for testing may be of two forms: individual complete contracts or continuation data. Continuation is defined in a way similar to spot prices; it is a series of prices made up of the nearest futures contract, excluding the delivery month. Continuation prices are practical if the system is generally traded on the nearest delivery month; if not, it may be a handicap. If you are trading new crop corn in the May preceding delivery, it would be difficult to attempt to take positions based on the movement of the July delivery. Although there is similarity between the two deliveries, there will be notable exceptions in both patterns and magnitude of movement.

For dynamic testing there are more choices. The techniques used for static testing can be used, or individual contracts can be tested. Since testing is repeated frequently, we can direct our studies to the delivery months being traded. The test map may show different parameters representing different moving averages for July corn and December corn based on their unique patterns. When retesting, we have the choice of testing the entire contract from the beginning, or testing a specified number of days from the most recent backwards. It should be remembered that the results of the mapping technique will tend toward slower moving averages as more data is accumulated.

The Scaling Index

The selection of the indices along the left edge and bottom of the test map will determine the extent of the test. Still using our moving average–percent stop-loss system, we could test every moving average from one to 10, or we could increase the span from 1 to 100 in steps of 10 (1, 11, 21, . . .). We would then discover that consecutive tests may have a total of 50, 40, 30, . . . completed trades for the testing period. It is important that the scaling result in an even distribution of completed trades; although there may be certain constraints placed on the testing (no more than 50 trades per year and no fewer than 3), severe restrictions may limit the field and make successful results impossible. There may not be any combination of parameters that performed well in the range of a 10- to 14-day moving average with a .5 to 1.0% stop-loss.

The scaling problem becomes more obvious when we consider the use of an exponentially smoothed moving average instead of a standard n-day average. The exponential method requires a smoothing constant between .0 and 1., which weights the value of the current day's price change with respect to prior prices. A value of 1. puts 100% weight on today's price, a value of .5 puts 50%, and so on. The scaling for the test map is easily selected to be equal intervals from .0 to 1. (not using the extremes) and is then expected to cover the full range of tests. But a simple conversion to moving average equivalents will show the fallacy of this scaling technique. An approximation for the straight moving average based on an exponential smoothing constant is

$$MA = \frac{1.5}{S}$$

where MA is the number of days in the straight moving average and S is the exponential smoothing constant $(0 \leqq S \leqq 1)$. We can construct a table of S and MA using equal intervals of S from .05 to .95:

S	MA	S	MA	S	MA	S	MA
.05	30	.30	5.00	.55	2.73	.80	1.88
.10	15	.35	4.30	.60	2.50	.85	1.76
.15	10	.40	3.75	.65	2.31	.90	1.67
.20	7.5	.45	3.33	.76	2.14	.95	1.58
.25	6.0	.50	3.00	.75	2.00		

It becomes obvious that 14 out of the 19 tests are concentrated on the equivalent of five or fewer moving average days, and four use fewer than two days. The results of this test map would show very little change for these values while the first few rows would have large discontinuities as the speed of the moving average jumps from 15 to 30 days; the error in the scaling is most readily seen in the distribution of trades generated from tests using these smoothing constants. Their values will vary considerably for smoothing constants from .05 to .25 and then will only change slightly afterward. To adjust for this error we can distribute the scaling values in a method complementary to the system being tested, in this case either exponentially or logarithmically with the smallest change near the lower values of smoothing constants and larger gaps as S becomes greater. The results will appear similar to the following table:

S	MA	S	MA	S	MA
.025	60	.038	40	.075	20
.027	55	.043	35	.100	15
.030	50	.050	30	.150	10
.033	45	.060	25	.300	5

It can be seen that this distribution will be more representative and useful for the application of exponential smoothing to the test map.

Shortcuts

The mapping system is an application of computer technology; such an approach could only be conceived and implemented with the speed of automation. The ideas of contours of success, retesting, precession, and predictability are a process of a new age of technology. However, there could be considerable time and cost involved in this type of testing method; it becomes reasonable for users to look for shortcuts.

The simplest approach to economizing is to test a smaller map with wider gaps between values of the scaling index. The resulting patterns should be sketchy but similar to a detailed test; then another test map can be created for the most successful area.

A shortcut which is frequently considered is representative of a manual testing approach. By selecting a particular column of the test map we have fixed a stop-loss criteria. We can proceed to test each moving average row from the top until we find a peak value, isolated by some drop of success before and after. Once this peak value is chosen we can move left or right looking for a peak value relative to the stop-loss criteria. This technique may work for isolating many of the best performance parameters, but conflicts with the philosophy of finding "plateaus" of success. It is also possible that minor peaks may cause this shortcut to stop looking for the best moving average too soon.

Variations in Testing and Analysis

Once the mapping system is used to test the performance of a trending system, it becomes evident that both the best and worst scores are clustered. The worst scores can present an argument equally as interesting as areas of good performance; they can identify situations for which the system being tested fails consistently. It is then up to the analyst to decide whether a consistent loser can be used as a winning method. Because of the way performance is calculated, the areas of losses may be due to the high commission burden of frequent trading, which will be equally as bad when trading contrary to, or "fading," the system.

It often happens that there is a clearly profitable, as well as clearly losing, area on the test map. Figure 5 shows what might happen when testing a double moving average system, where the fastest trends of both averages are at the top left and the slowest at the bottom right. The map shows the area of worst performance where both moving averages are fast, and the area of best performance for slow trends. One viable plan for using the information in this test is to follow the long-term trend, given by the slow moving averages (best score) but to time the entry

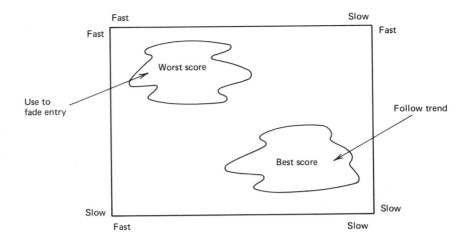

FIGURE 5
Dual use of test map.

into the trade by fading the recommendation given by the results of the worst score.

When a buy or sell signal is generated by the two moving averages selected by the best score, we can assume that the long-term trend has been determined accurately. But the trader may prefer a better timing indicator than a slow movement of prices across a long-term trendline. Signals given by long-term indicators are usually followed by a price adjustment, where an entry could have been achieved at a better price. The signal given by the moving averages generating the worse score were representative of fast price movement. Since they were usually wrong, we can consider them antitrend indicators, or "overbought-oversold" signals. When a buy signal occurs we can sell, and when a sell signal occurs we buy. To incorporate the double moving average system with the best and worst sets of averages, we buy and sell only when the best score trend is long or short, respectively, but at the time when the worse score trend indicates to sell or buy (the opposite signal).

Point-and-Figure Testing

The testing of the point-and-figure method of charting is an obvious application of the mapping system. We can test the size of each point-and-figure box along the left of the map and the number of boxes for a

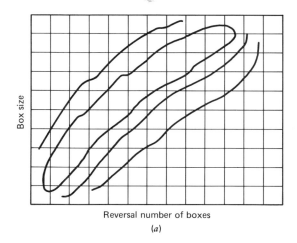

Reversal number of boxes

(a)

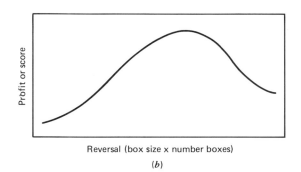

Reversal (box size x number boxes)

(b)

FIGURE 6
Point-and-figure mapping strategy.

reversal (indicating a trend change) along the bottom of the map. Figure 6a shows that the expected pattern of results is symmetric, extending across the diagonal drawn from the top left to the bottom right corners. In this example we consider the fastest trend change to be in the upper left and the slowest in the lower right corners.

The reason for the symmetry is that performance is fairly constant for equal reversal values, regardless of its distribution into box size and number of boxes to generate a reversal. If we start testing grains by allowing multiples of 1¢ box sizes, we get 1, 2, 3, . . . from the top down on the left of the map. The number of boxes in a reversal will also be 1, 2, 3, . . . from left to right along the bottom. Therefore, the corner box (top left) represents a 1¢ box with a 1-box reversal, or a total reversal value of 1¢. It can be seen that a 12¢ total reversal value can be the combination of 1¢ × 12, 2¢ × 6, 3¢ × 4, 4¢ × 3, 6¢ × 2, or 12¢ × 1. A change of direction, which is the most important single event in determining a buy or sell signal, will occur at exactly the same time with any of the combinations. After the trend change, the smaller box size will allow more frequent extension of the charts. The results of all the combinations will be similar, and therefore the best performance contour in the test map will be symmetric.

Because of the symmetry of the test map, the results can be expressed differently to supplement the analysis of the performance. By plotting the average results of all combinations of the same total reversal value, we get a curve similar to the one shown in Figure 6b. The curve indicates that there is continuity of reversal value and performance, with a well-defined peak. We can use the best results of this technique to isolate the symmetric strip in the test map relating to the total reversal value. The average area scoring method discussed previously will then isolate the best combination of box size and reversal within that symmetric contour. The results will be parameters selected for best performance using a multiple-continuity criteria.

Summary

An important concern when using a new testing structure, such as the mapping system, is the possibility of overtesting. It is very likely that massive testing will isolate successful historic results that have no predictive qualities. Because of this possibility, the philosophy of the mapping system is to concentrate on wide areas of success rather than peaks. If 30% of all tests appearing on the map are successful, we have more confidence in the overall method. It may be comforting to generate various statistics about the total testing results as displayed on the map: the mean profit, reliability, number of trades, score, and the standard deviation of the results. For soybeans tested on a moving average system using one-year intervals for 1970–1977, it was shown that the average profit was 140% and the standard deviation 60%. That means it is improbable that soybean trading would show a loss during any one year, using a typical moving average system, and gives the user confidence in the credibility of his own method.

When making changes to the trading model that is being tested on the mapping system, the summary statistics are a good means for determining improvements in the technique. Although peak performance may improve, the average of all performance may decline, indicating sharper test peaks and perhaps a finer tuning of the method. Improvement in the average would imply an improvement in the technique over most conditions.

The mapping system is still a new concept of testing and will probably be changed beyond recognition as computers and calculators become part of our everyday life. It introduces a solution that is part of our new environment rather than an adaptation of an older, manual method that has been speeded up through automation. It can be used to test the relationship of any two variables provided there is incremental continuity in both directions; it can also be used for long- and short-term testing with historic and predictive results. It is a tool, not a system, but it may be essential for the research analyst.

PART **4**

COMMERCIAL

If a commodity producer or speculator had a 20/20 crystal ball, the following discussion would be superfluous. He could simply gaze into the sphere, observe the date and level of the highest price this season, and when that date and price arrived—sell.

Until such crystal balls are available, however, the dilemma of when and at what price to sell must be dealt with by other means. The importance of these decisions is directly proportional to the size (and nature) of the position. A one-contract speculator may be more willing and able to gamble on attaining the highest price than, say, a farmer, who may be staking the viability of his means of livelihood on the price he receives for his large crop.

Conventional wisdom calls for a marketing goal of average pricing, achieved by selling equal amounts at equal intervals over a specified time span. This earns the seller the mean price and precludes his having to make a subjective determination of the best price or time to sell. Like most conventional wisdom, however, this approach can be improved on through careful analysis of what we are dealing with.

The foundation for Mr. Kaufman's commodity selling model is a discussion of the nature and significance of price distribution. To this he adds considerations of price volatility; variations in the number, size, and timing of sales; seasonality; and risk/reward ratios. The resulting model is a fascinating and innovative method for determining optimum sales strategy.

COMMODITY SELLING MODEL
A Theory of Price
Distribution

PERRY J. KAUFMAN

The purpose of this discussion is to introduce a new selling model, of a generalized nature, that uses the commodity futures markets and cash markets in an integrated way to improve returns on sales at little or no increase in risk to the user. The extent of usage of the model and its effective returns depend on the price patterns of the futures markets during the period to which it is applied. It is a practical model, since it permits the user to sell his product at regular intervals in the cash market, avoiding abnormally large sales at one time. Large single cash market sales, if possible at all, may be taken at such a substantial discount that the advantage of a high price may be forfeited. The model is expected to return near-average prices in the worst situation and improve returns from 5% to 15% above the average during a year of normal performance. It is applied, as price patterns permit, with varying frequency during the year. The model can be applied exclusively to the cash market, if required.

The most frequently recommended method of marketing any product is one of *average pricing*. To get an average price it is only necessary to sell equal quantities of a product at equal intervals and thus avoid any subjective determination of the best price or the best time to sell. A farmer may sell one-sixth of his crop every two months or one-quarter of the crop every three months to get an average price; a processor or manufacturer maintaining constant activity may sell a fixed part of his inventory or production weekly to get an average. By not attempting to predict future price movements the producer gives up the possibility of getting either the highest or lowest price of a time period; he gets the mean price. But where does the mean lie relative to the price range for the year?

Distribution of Prices

Tables 1a and 1b show evaluations of the price distribution of both wheat and platinum futures contracts during the 10-year period from 1969 through 1978. The highest and lowest contract prices are given, along with the midpoint, mean of the daily closing prices, standard deviation, and the relationship of the mean to the midpoint, expressed in percentages. For these years the average price of the contract was consistently below the midpoint of the range. This shows that the distribution of prices is skewed toward lower price levels.

TABLE 1a PRICE DISTRIBUTION: JULY WHEAT

	Prices				*Distribution*		
Year	*High*	*Low*	*Midpoint*	*Average*	*% Average <Midpoint*	*1σ*	*1σ / (H-L)*
1969	142⅛	124½	133.3	132.4	−5.1	3.5	19.4%
1970	144⅜	129¾	137.1	136.8	−2.1	2.2	15.0%
1971	168⅞	148½	158.7	157.7	−4.9	4.1	20.1%
1972	153¼	135⅝	144.4	143.4	−5.7	3.6	20.4%
1973	304	178⅛	241.1	229.0	−9.6	27.9	22.2%
1974	585	287	436.0	413.8	−7.5	58.7	19.7%
1975	509	293	401.0	392.6	−3.9	63.8	29.5%
1976	440	334½	387.3	375.8	−10.9	27.6	26.2%
1977	377½	233	305.3	291.7	−9.4	34.3	23.7%
1978	341	243½	292.3	285.0	−7.5	23.7	24.3%

Further distortion of the distribution is obvious when looking at the exceptional situation in January 1975 platinum, where the average daily price was 21% lower than the midpoint. This is to say, although platinum prices ranged from \$314 to \$159 per ounce that year, the mean price was only 29% from the bottom, or \$204. The standard deviation of \$30.40 indicates that approximately 65% of the prices fell between \$173.60 and \$234.40 and that the lowest price is only \$44.90 below the mean, or less than 1.5 standard deviations. Then about 80% of the prices are in the lowest \$90 range, and 20% of the prices are in the upper \$65 range. The possibility of getting a sale price of \$249 strictly by chance is only 1 out of 5. A price distribution representing the 1975 platinum contract is shown in Figure 1.

The past 10 years of wheat prices (Table 1a) show results not as extreme as platinum but as consistent. In other studies it was shown that not all situations resulted in daily averages below the midpoint. When prices experience a long upward move and hold at higher price levels for a season, a distortion will occur, resulting in an average price above the midpoint; when considered over a longer time period, this distortion can be eliminated.

Understanding the significance of the nature of price distribution is important for the producer and the selling model. It means that higher-

TABLE 1b PRICE DISTRIBUTION: JANUARY PLATINUM

	Prices				*Distribution*		
Year	*High*	*Low*	*Midpoint*	*Average*	*% Average <Midpoint*	*1σ*	*1σ (H-L)*
1970	243.0	153.0	198.0	197.2	− .9	32.0	35.5%
1971	195.5	112.5	154.0	152.2	− 2.0	20.6	24.8%
1972	153.9	97.6	125.8	117.1	−15.4	10.3	18.3%
1973	163.7	98.0	130.9	122.9	−12.2	17.9	27.2%
1974	193.1	137.5	165.3	158.3	−12.6	11.7	21.0%
1975	314.5	159.5	237.0	204.4	−21.0	30.4	19.6%
1976	230.0	141.0	185.5	169.6	−17.9	21.5	24.2%
1977	192.8	141.8	167.3	160.9	−12.5	10.5	20.6%
1978	186.9	146.3	166.6	165.0	− 3.9	8.6	21.2%
1979	289.5	160.1	224.8	223.6	− .9	36.1	27.9%

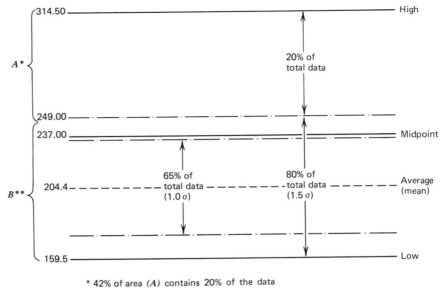

FIGURE 1
Platinum—January 1975.

than-average prices occur in substantial magnitude but with short duration. Action must be well calculated and expedient. The classic decision-making process of the unsophisticated farmer is an excellent example of the wrong approach. A farmer, aware of his costs, will set a price goal for his crop sales. After waiting, prices rise to his objective, but the farmer fails to execute his sale, choosing to wait to see how much higher prices will go. He will continue to wait optimistically until prices have reversed from their highs by such a large amount that the price peak is obvious. He then knows where the "top" is and will intend to sell when it is again reached. Unfortunately, that top is usually not attained a second time; if it were, the farmer may again stand optimistically aside waiting for still higher prices. The farmer traditionally sells either when he needs the income or when prices have fallen to such a depressed level that he is certain they will never rise again. Neither situation will benefit him.

The time to sell is when prices are obviously higher than normal and moving up. Since those occasions do not usually last long, a hasty decision at a high price will usually be a successful one. Later, a more systematic approach will be presented.

The nature of price distribution shows that timing is of great importance in pricing. Opportunities exist for improving a selling price; these occasions cannot be realized by selling at equal intervals as proposed by the average pricing method. We must next consider the quantities to be sold when the opportunities arise.

Variations on Quantities Sold

It is evident that even average pricing returns the expected only if equal quantities are sold at each opportunity. The "average" could be greatly distorted if unequal quantities were sold; it would then be termed a weighted average. In a weighted average any one term could be rendered meaningless by giving it substantially small weight while another term is heavily weighted in significance. For example, a farmer sells one-tenth of his corn crop at the season's high of $3.50 per bushel. For the remainder of the year prices drift lower and bottom at $2.50, giving a midpoint of $3.00 and an average of $2.85. The farmer manages to sell the remainder of his crop at the average price of $2.85. But one lot at $3.50 and nine lots at $2.85 only resulted in $2.91½ per bushel, not even the midpoint, although the farmer was able to pick the season high for his first sale. The quantities sold (9 to 1) caused the net price to be heavily weighted toward the average.

The number of sales themselves play an important role in the relationship of net sales price to average price. The more often you sell and the smaller the lot, the closer you must get to the mean price. Even the best prices cannot be distinguished from the average if there are too many sales. As an example we define a *Utopian sales model*. This model has the advantage of being able to select the highest price of any time interval as a selling price, although in reality it would have been impossible to have known what price to choose. We will always sell equal quantities of the product at the highest price within a predetermined interval; the intervals will be continuous over the life of the futures contract being analyzed. When the results are accumulated for various interval lengths, we will compare the results of these variations in optimum average pricing.

In our example we will use a selection of four 1978 futures contracts: November soybeans, December wheat, December silver (Comex), and December gold (Comex). For each interval chosen we will find the highest, lowest, and average prices. Figure 2, using the left scale to

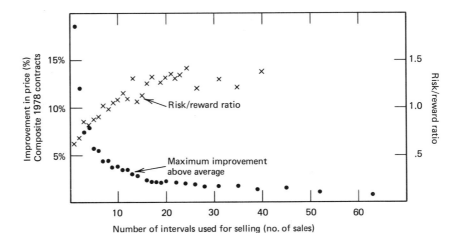

FIGURE 2
Results of Utopian sales model.

represent percentage improvement above the average, shows the relationship of the optimum selling price to the average daily price for varying intervals of all four contracts. It is easily seen that the fewer the sales, the greater the opportunity for improvement. The best possible return for this test was the single highest price, 18.6% above the average. This optimum price declined rapidly as the number of intervals increased, until it reached a stable rate of 1% above the average. That 1% base indicates the relationship of the average daily high to the average daily closing price.

The rapid decline in improvement reaches about 2.3% (or 1.3% above the relative base) at 16 intervals or sales for the contract. From this we can conclude that 16 or more sales, distributed over equal intervals of equal quantities, will return an average price. Since a Utopian selection of price yields a maximum potential improvement of 1.3%, an average selection must return less. It seems that any serious attempt to select better timing points for selling a product is offset by the nature of price distribution that permits smaller price fluctuations in shorter time intervals. An attempt to improve prices must therefore commit to fewer sales of larger quantities to yield the best return for the effort expended.

We can further analyze the number of sales that offer the best opportunity for high returns by calculating the risk and reward for the seller as follows:

Risk is the difference between the average closing price and the lowest price of the contract for each interval, averaged for all intervals of the same span.

Reward is the difference between the highest price and the average closing price of the contract for each interval, averaged for all intervals of the same span.

Because of the distortion in the distribution of prices discussed previously, we can expect larger intervals to have a lower risk/reward ratio, that is, the highest prices should be farther from the mean than the lowest prices for the same time interval. When short intervals are used, this pattern may not have adequate time to develop. The longer the interval, the greater will be the approach to the ideal distribution. Figure 2 shows the results of the composite test of the four commodities selected. The right scale represents the ratio of risk to reward; when it is below 1.00 the risk is proportionately less than the reward; when above 1.00, the risk is greater. The bottom scale (horizontal x axis) indicates the number of intervals or sales in the fixed length of the contracts tested. The far left is one interval, or the highest price of the entire contract; two intervals indicates two equal divisions of approximately six months and so on. As you proceed further to the right, the intervals become smaller and more frequent and therefore approach the constant relationship of the daily highs to the daily closing prices, about 1%. Some sample data and calculations for December '78 gold appear in Table 2.

TABLE 2   RISK/REWARD EVALUATION: DECEMBER 1978 GOLD
Midpoint = 192.15, Average = 186.44

No. of Intervals	Length of Interval	Maximum Price	Maximum Above Average	Minimum Price	Minimum Below Average	Max-Min Difference	Risk/ Reward
1	14 mo.	224.60	38.16	153.50	34.94	71.10	.916
2	7 mo.	210.55	24.11	163.15	23.29	47.40	.966
3	5 mo.	207.10	20.66	171.07	15.37	36.03	.744
4	4 mo.	205.62	19.18	173.90	12.54	32.40	.654
5	3 mo.	202.08	15.56	174.22	11.57	27.86	.744
7	2 mo.	196.50	10.06	175.87	10.57	20.63	1.051
14	1 mo.	192.87	6.42	177.92	8.52	14.95	1.330

The table shows that the highest absolute price could only be achieved by a single sale. The most favorable risk/reward ratio, however, occurred when there were four equal intervals, after which the risk again began to increase. As the intervals become smaller, the risk/reward ratio will approach one. It must be concluded that the best combination of risk and opportunity is neither the single attempt to pick the highest price, nor the frequent sale of small quantities; it is a few sales of moderately large quantities. This confirms the two other analyses of price distribution: that the skewness toward higher prices is infrequent and that the ideal improvement in sales price is greatest when fewer sales are affected. It shows both timing and quantity are important to the ultimate selling price.

Selection of Sales

We have now determined that the *average price* is not as glamorous nor can the returns be as high as we would have originally expected. In addition, an intelligent guess at a potentially high sales price offers more reward than risk. From our discussions, we set our own goal at three to five sales; this will permit the seller more than one opportunity in the event the first sale is not successful. We can now look at a simple method for improving the selection process.

The system to be described has two primary features: a moving average and a volatility measure. The moving average is to be used in the classic sense, to determine the average price of a commodity over some specific time interval. This interval may be defined in terms of the production cycle of the product as well as the length of the maximum commitment acceptable to the seller. Remembering that each sale will commit a large portion of production at the current price, it is evident that the moving average must be of such a speed as to generate not more than our optimum number of sell signals. After all, if 25% of production is being sold on each of four signals, the occurrence of five or more signals within a production cycle becomes an impossible condition. Similarly, the occasion of no signals will cause the model to be useless. The problem of uncertainty in the number of selling signals that will be generated during the selling cycle is discussed later. At this time we examine only the technique for generating signals.

Using a selling cycle of one year, we can consider the problems of a farmer with a single-crop production, where the crop is perishable, such as potatoes. We then limit the possibilities of extended carry-over due to the storability of the product. Although we always have the possibility of advance sales of the old or new crop and physical sale of the old crop, we discuss only the simple case of cash sales of a stored product over a one-year cycle and do not intermix the marketing of two crops. The techniques discussed can be applied to varying proportions of two crop years.

The moving average selected will tell us whether the current market price is higher or lower than the average price over a prior interval equal to the production cycle or some smaller (shorter) part of the production cycle. In a simple way this can be determined by comparing the current price with the moving average, so that a 90-day moving average value of $7.00 per bushel of soybeans, compared to a current cash price of $7.50 per bushel indicates that prices are now 7.1% above the average. Having made this sale, we are faced with the problem of when to make the next sale. If the prices continue higher we may have a better opportunity in two or three days; a price advance to $8.00 may only move the 90-day average to $7.10 and therefore allow a sale of 90¢ above the average. The problem that immediately arises is the frequency of allowable sales and the percentage above the average that affords the best opportunity for high returns.

Minimum Time Between Sales

We have already spent most of our effort in discussing the frequency of sales. Since the objective of the selling model is to have only about four sales per year, it is important that sales do not occur too closely together and eliminate opportunities for sales at another time. A possible filter for frequent sales is simply a compulsory lag between sales. In brief testing it was shown that a two-week minimum span between occurrences was satisfactory.

Alternately, a seasonal bias can be assigned to sell signals. The harvest months, traditionally having the most depressed prices, may be completely eliminated from potential sell signals; the early spring and later summer months, which usually experience larger price fluctuations because of planting and weather expectations, may be more heavily weighted. By varying or weighting the size of the sale by the seasonal distribution, the sale of the total crop can be executed with more frequent sell signals.

Price Volatility

A more important factor in signaling a selling opportunity is the extent of price movement above the moving average. To measure this we use the concept of volatility. We define the volatility of a specific commodity as the magnitude of price fluctuation from highest to lowest price over a fixed interval.* It is intuitively obvious that volatility must increase as the fixed interval of measurement increases, since prices have a greater opportunity to vary over a longer time span. It is not as obvious, but nevertheless true, that there is a direct relationship between the magnitude of fluctuation and the price level. When prices are at base levels, near econometric lows, the volatility is correspondingly low. As prices move higher, because of anticipation of increased demand (or reduced supply), the volatility also increases. The farther the prices move above the base price (the point where the volatility is zero), the greater the latitude for fluctuation. It seems clear that at \$6.00 per bushel, wheat prices will be substantially more volatile than at \$2.50 per bushel. For any fixed interval of measurement, the volatility can be reasonably approximated by a linear function:

$$V = B + S \cdot P$$

where V is the volatility at price P
P is the price level
B is the base price constant $(P{=}0)$
S is the slope, or angle of increase of
volatility magnitude as price increases.

For wheat, this relationship is as follows:

1-month intervals: $V_1(P) = -10.8 + .077P$

2-month intervals: $V_2(P) = -12.6 + .097P$

3-month intervals: $V_3(P) = -18.5 + .133P$

We can combine the volatility function with a moving average to define an extreme upward move, also called an *overbought* condition. We will attempt to structure the combined functions of moving average and volatility to isolate relative price peaks, as shown in Figure 3.

The moving average line MA represents the actual average of the prior

---

* A complete discussion of this relationship can be found in "The Price–Volatility Relationship," pp. 99–113.

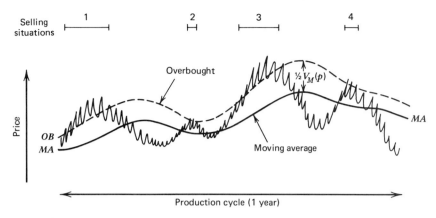

FIGURE 3
Identifying price peaks.

N days; the upper line varies in distance from the moving average, based on the volatility function $V_M(P)$, the volatility measured over span M at price level P on day t (since the price is actually P_t). As prices increase, $V_M(P)$ increases. Violation of the combined indicator line OB gives the overbought condition and signals a time for selling. The objective of the OB line is to isolate the optimum number of peak price periods over the selling cycle, relating to the optimum number of sales determined by the risk/reward analysis. If we intend to sell four times during a season, each time with an equal 25% of production, then our OB line must isolate no more than four peaks.

Other volatility functions could be used to create the OB line. Instead of the generalized function, $V_M(P)$, we could simply measure the price fluctuations from high to low for some fixed interval, as the past 90 days or the past selling cycle. A simple histogram (frequency distribution) of prices during the interval selected for measurement of volatility would allow determination of the standard deviation. We can then create the OB line by adding 1.5 or 2.0 times the standard deviation of the volatility. In doing this we have an empirical measure of probability of occurrence of the volatility and may be able to fine-tune the location of the OB line.

Delay Between Sales

We can now go back to the previous discussion of the minimum time between sales and consider the illustration of Figure 3. The peaks isolated by the *OB* line may remain above the line for an extended period of time, as seen in selling situations 1 and 3. It is necessary to introduce a delay between selling opportunities, otherwise each day that prices remain above the *OB* line could indicate additional sales. One possibility would be to permit only one sale on each unique upward penetration of the *OB* line. Instead, in our model we do not allow any sale within close proximity to a prior sale, and we relate that time delay to the length of the selling cycle. By doing this we restrict frequent sales that might occur on marginal penetration of the *OB* line, as well as continuous selling of a sustained high price.

The time delay permits the seller to initiate more than one sale when prices remain above the *OB* line for long intervals. Since this is likely to happen during extended bull moves and during seasonal rallies, it is advantageous to be able to sell more than once. For selling cycles of one year, delays of two to four weeks, depending on the commodity, should be considered. It is important to choose the longest possible delay, since the most serious problem faced is that of exhausting your sales too early in the selling cycle.

Relating the Quantity Sold to the Seasonal Distribution

It would not appear to be a violation of the previous discussion of frequency and quantity of sales, if the quantities were weighted to allow larger sales during the times of the year in which the seasonality usually causes higher prices. It seems easy to justify the creation of a seasonal selling distribution for corn which reduces the quantity available for sale during the October–November harvest and increases sales quantities during the summer months. This method could still satisfy the main premise of the model by restricting the total number of sales to three to five of substantial quantities. A possible distribution might be two sales of $12\frac{1}{2}\%$ each during the harvest months and three sales of 25% each during other seasons.

The normal seasonal distributions would make this an improvement most of the time, but sellers may find the past few years enough of an exception to reject it. In 1976 corn prices moved higher throughout the harvest season, peaking in the first part of 1977 and then moving steadily lower all year, ending with depressed prices during 1977 harvest. During that one-year cycle only a small quantity would have been sold during the late 1976 months and perhaps only one additional sale in early 1977. No other opportunity would have materialized for the remainder of the crop year. The determination of proper delay or lag time should permit multiple sales at seasonal highs without restricting the time of year in which sales opportunities will occur (see Figure 4).

Possible Price Patterns

As structured, the selling model should indicate sales opportunities on rallies in price. The overbought line measures the anticipated size of the rally. Since the *OB* line is substantially above the moving average, you are always assured of an above-average price for that period. Figure 5 shows two basic pattern variations that are most likely to generate selling opportunities. Note that in Figure 4 the moving average line will rise as prices rise, and the *OB* line will move away from *MA* at higher price levels. Penetration of the *OB* line causes a sell signal; following penetration of the *OB* line high prices should deteriorate, leaving the prior sale at a favorable price.

Figure 5a shows a more complex situation. The first sale is generated as in Figure 4, but prices fail to return to lower levels. This occasionally happens when the economics of an industry change suddenly, or when a critical shortage cannot be eliminated in the near future. A lasting change in the price of a commodity is not a frequent occurrence and will not affect the success of the model. It only means that the first portion sold will be closer to the average price for the remaining part of the selling cycle. As seen in Figure 5a, the moving average and the *OB* line will then adjust to new levels, and subsequent sales will be at new relative peaks.

The overbought condition applies in declining markets as well as rising ones. Figure 5b shows that rallies in sustained bear markets will also generate sell signals. The only situation for which no signal will be indicated is a sustained steady movement with no peaks.

Application of the Sales Model

There are some obvious problems in applying the sales model which can be eliminated by introducing the use of the futures markets. The problems of importance are:

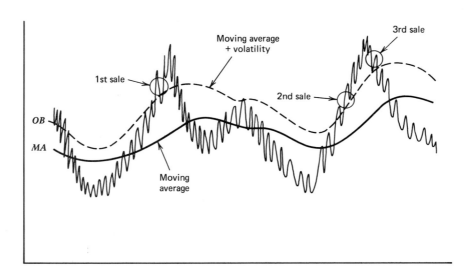

FIGURE 4
Seller's hedge—multiple sales in a single peak.

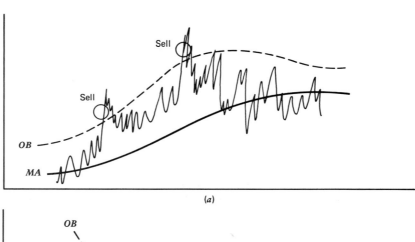

(a)

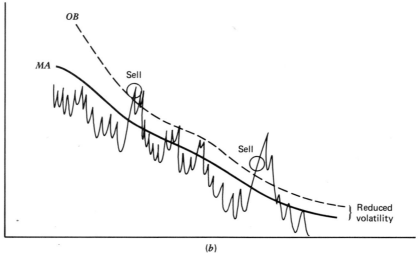

(b)

FIGURE 5
Price pattern variations.
(a) Changes in economics. (b) Bear market rallies.

1. The inability to sell large quantities of production in the cash market.

2. The lack of a forward cash market during all or some seasons.

3. The discount that may be taken by selling in the cash market at a time of immediate oversupply or with an adverse basis.

4. The possibility that selling opportunities as generated by the model may not account for 100% of production or that no selling opportunities may occur.

The use of the futures market, where possible, can be a solution to all these problems. It is first essential that the futures market used relates directly to your product. A simple correlation of local cash prices to spot prices (nearest futures contract) will give you a good idea of this relationship. The futures market, in the economic sense, is a perfect market. It offers liquidity and the ability to sell at the quoted price in quantities varying from modest to high. It provides a foundation for the forward pricing of deliverable grain; it creates a forward market for livestock, for which only daily physical sales are possible; and it fills the seasonal void in commodities such as potatoes that have few delivery contracts offered to the farmer prior to the harvesting of the fall crop. The futures market allows you to select the time of delivery and take advantage of your ability to store when prices are favorable.

Sales using futures avoid the unrealistic problem of trying to sell large quantities of a product at one time. The futures market will absorb available supply offered for sale at the point of extreme upward price movement, as indicated by the *OB* line, where prices are moving higher rapidly and have not yet shown signs of halting or reversing. It is evident that demand exceeds supply and buyers have not reached their saturation point. For this reason it is important that the sale of large quantities always takes place during the initial upward price thrust. We do not want to be the farmer, mentioned earlier, who is still waiting for prices to return to their obvious high to execute his sale. For these reasons sales must be placed at predetermined levels as prices move up.

Incomplete Sales

The most important use of futures is to avoid the possibility of incomplete sale of production. The selling model relies on price rallies to generate an overbought condition. A gradual deterioration of prices, as seen in 1977 corn, may not signal any sales. During that season there were no rallies in the declining price pattern. The futures market can be used to take advantage of selling opportunities as indicated by the model, while selling of physicals continue at regular intervals in the cash market. If the model fails to generate any sell signals, full production has still been sold at an average price. Signals generated by the selling model will improve on the average price to the extent of the portion of production to which it applies.

Positions taken in the futures markets according to this plan are termed a traditional hedge. They are liquidated only as they correspond to the cash sale of the physical product. For example, a copper dealer with an annual inventory of 3 million pounds (120 contracts of 25,000 pounds each) gets a signal to presell 25% of his inventory. He must then sell 30 contracts in the futures market. To do this properly he must distribute his sales such that the hedge positions can be closed out at regular intervals throughout the selling cycle. By lifting the short-hedge positions at regular intervals we can get an average price, as shown in the principles of price distribution discussed earlier. The copper dealer will then get an above average price for his sale and an average price for buying back the hedge position; the difference between the two will be profit. Had we closed out the hedge positions over a shorter interval, we would not be assured of an average price. (See Figure 6.)

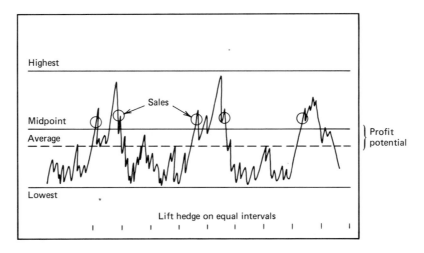

FIGURE 6
Seller's hedge—application of the
sales model using the futures markets.

The copper dealer using futures has a choice of entering all his hedge positions in one delivery month a full cycle removed (e.g., one year deferred) or distributing the 30 contracts equally among all delivery months, which may be more effective. Hedge positions are then closed out at regular intervals, beginning with the position nearest to delivery. If the deferred delivery months are too thinly traded for sizeable hedging quantities it may be necessary to assign those contracts to a more nearby month and roll them into the deferred month when liquidity improves. An advantage of copper futures, as with other nonseasonal, nonperishable commodities, is the high correlation of price movements of different delivery months to one another. A sell indication in any month will usually be valid for the others.

The grains and livestock present a problem of variation in the patterns of delivery months. The grains often differ between old and new crops, while livestock vary by production cycle and season. In the case of grains, it is unlikely that a major move upward centered in new crop fundamental information, such as poor anticipated yield, will not affect the old crop similarly. The initial emphasis is concentrated on the specific crop concerned, but after a short period of distortion, the old crop will reflect a similar demand. Much of this has been discussed by Holbrook Working in *A Theory of Anticipatory Prices.**
Our concern is in how to use a futures-based pricing structure to implement the sales model. If August soybean prices rally because of near-term shortage prior to harvest of the new crop, the sale of 25% to be distributed over an entire crop year may be unreasonable if the deferred months have not yet reflected the nearby rally. An old crop sell signal that occurs in the month of July based on either cash prices or August futures can only be hedged using August delivery, and it therefore allows no more than one month, or $1/12$ of the annual production to be hedged. This quantity is too small to be significant.

The only solution for the grain hedger is to consider old and new crop prices as distinct. By allocating 50% of production to be sold prior to harvest, we also have 50% of the crop to be stored for cash sales through next season. We can then use an analysis of current cash prices, relating to August futures during the months of November through August (when there is an old crop in storage). The new crop pricing will use the November futures price whenever it is available. We have then avoided the variation of old and new crop prices by considering them separately; in doing this we have extended the marketing time of

* *Selected Writings of Holbrook Working*, Chicago Board of Trade, Chicago, 1977.

a single crop to about 20 months.   (December to November for new
crop and then December through August for old crop.)   Opportunities
arising in either old or new crop can be taken equally.

The livestock problem may be considered in a manner similar to the
old-new crop grains.   Midwestern livestock production, which is seasonal, can be treated by proper selection of one or two delivery months
corresponding to specific production periods.   Continuous production
operations may find that the simplest application is one of following
two or three contracts representing seasonal variation, such as December and July hogs.   Applying too many contracts will not enable large
sales in any one month.   The user is reminded that the diversification
into more than one futures contract is for convenience and protection
against price moves that are either out of phase or of varying magnitude;
it is probable that a sell signal will be generated simultaneously in both
old and new crops or in most months of livestock delivery at the same
time.

Practical Limitations

There are two obvious limitations in the use of this hedging method.
The first is the ability of the futures market to absorb the necessary
quantity of sales.   Since sales are infrequent and of large quantity,
the less liquid commodity as well as the extremely large traders may require scaling into a position over a number of days.   Since prices should
be advancing during the selling period, most sales should be concluded
successfully.   When lifting the hedge position, trades can be distributed
as broadly as possible and liquidated in small numbers over regular
intervals, even daily if necessary.   The only difficulty is in entry.   If
markets are too thin for the total desired hedge, profit potential may
still be adequate based on the reduced quantity that the market will
absorb.

The second concern is the capital required to maintain the hedge position until it is lifted.   It is possible for prices to continue to rise through
a season or production cycle.   Sales entered at what was originally a
peak may ultimately be lifted at an average loss.   Consider the most
likely situation of advancing prices that remain at the next high level
before declining.   On the first move up we hedge one-third of the annual
production of corn at $2.50 per bushel.   Prices continue to advance
until they stabilize at $2.75.   On another advance we hedge one-third
at $3.00 before prices decline to $2.75 again; the remainder of the

season they drift slowly back to $2.50, with no additional opportunities for hedging the final one-third of production.

The first one-third hedged at $2.50 was lifted over the balance of the season, resulting in an average liquidation price of $2.70, a 20¢ loss. The second one-third was also lifted at $2.75 for a 25¢ profit on an equal amount. The net result was a 5¢ profit on one-third of production. During this entire period, cash sales of equal amounts were made at equal intervals to get an average price on the physical commodity and not saturate the market, build inventory, or anticipate a specific price move. After the first hedge was entered and prices continued to advance, it was necessary to finance that position up to the high price of $3.00, or 50¢ per bushel. Since we are lifting those hedge positions regularly from the moment they are entered, we can assume that it was only necessary to finance the 50¢ loss on one-half of the original hedge position, or one-sixth of production. At the same time the remaining two-thirds of production, which has not been hedged, has been gaining in value, and the cash sales are receiving a higher average price. Although we lost 20¢ per bushel on the first hedge position, the average sale price of the corresponding physical commodity was higher than the entry price of the hedge position, reducing the net loss to under 20¢. At the same time the balance of production is benefiting from the increased price.

Financial demands become greatest if the price increase is not followed by a decline, and all three hedge positions result in net losses for the entire annual production. Although this is a rare occurrence, we should consider the implications. It is always true that if prices continued to advance, the best strategy would have been to do nothing and wait for the last possible moment to sell. That generally is not a good business practice. Continued high prices will carry into the futures contracts following the current season or production cycle, and the rules for hedging can be extended so that new opportunities are taken up in the next season's production, guaranteeing a high return. This process should be followed as long as prices advance and futures contracts are available for hedging of deferred production. This plan makes the assumption that prices will eventually decline or stabilize at a higher level and at that time a sufficiently large hedge position would have been maintained to benefit from the highest prices for an additional full production cycle. The producer will ultimately benefit from the higher value of the production which is fully hedged at the beginning of the price decline.

PART 5

EXPERIENCE

Todd Lofton *(also known as Edgar K. Lofton, Jr.) has been a career naval officer and naval aviator, a professional writer, and a futures trader for some 20 years. In 1971, with Leon Rose, he founded* Commodities *magazine, for which he served as publisher and editor until early 1975, when the publication was acquired by its present owner. A past member and floor trader on the Chicago Board Options Exchange, Mr. Lofton today acts as a consultant to several large firms who are involved with the futures markets.*

The fundamental approach to commodities markets does not work all the time, even within its own framework. Occasionally it is not possible to account for all the factors that affect prices; even some major influences are overlooked when they take on new perspective. The dramatic currency fluctuations of the past year are an example of a minor influence that became a major one.

Technical analysis includes areas of short-term trading and timing that are not applicable to fundamental analysis. Although cash-market influences get immediate short-term reactions from the futures markets, these reactions are behavioral. They occasionally result in what is normally expected by the unsophisticated observer, but these movements often seem to overreact or act completely contrary to the expected fundamental reaction. Technical analysis has become the accepted way to evaluate these price movements.

In this article by Todd Lofton, published in Commodities *magazine in May 1977, we see a fascinating and perceptive idea which adds further justification to technical analysis.*

THE PSYCHOLOGICAL VALUE OF TECHNICAL ANALYSIS

TODD LOFTON

If you have been trading commodities for very long, you have no doubt made the acquaintance of technical analysis. Technical analysis is the study of the markets themselves . . . of the action of prices, trading volume, and open interest and what clues their behavior can give us about where prices will be tomorrow. Depending on whom you talk to, technical analysis is everything from a useless pacifier to the only reliable way to trade commodities successfully.

The most popular tool for technical analysis of the commodity markets is the daily price chart, preferably one that also shows daily trading volume and open interest in charted form. Moving along the scale toward more esoteric technical tools, you find point-and-figure charts. Beyond these are increasingly complex ways to measure and index the data: on-balance volume and open interest, price momentum indices, mathematical oscillators, moving averages, time cycles, numerical series, optimization, and on until you reach a point where only a computer can masticate the information and formulas in time for the conclusions to be of any use.

Specific Quantities

One important attribute of technical analysis is that it is quantitative. It deals with numbers—with high, low, and closing prices, the number of contracts traded and open interest levels expressed numerically. Another is that the information is readily available. Many metropolitan newspapers carry these data daily. And the information is limited. Although there are many ways the information can be manipulated, the basic input comprises three simple groups of numbers.

These attributes alone account for a fringe benefit of technical analysis that is rarely, if ever, mentioned: its psychological value.

Few of us make any decisions in this life without some prior knowledge of what is likely to happen as a result. If we don't already have clues as to the probable outcome of our decision, we go looking for some. If we're thinking about having a backyard picnic, we check the weather forecast. If we're getting ready for an extended automobile trip, we gather road maps and maybe a catalog of motels or campsites enroute. If we're in the market for a new color television set, we might review the consumer magazines to see which one offers us the most for our money, then check prices at several stores before we decide.

The importance of such *a priori* knowledge is directly proportional to the amount of money or personal convenience involved. A rained-out picnic is one thing. A $700, 24-inch-screen lemon is another. Considering the amounts of money at stake and the dramatic changes in equity possible in trading commodities, a great deal of accurate *a priori* knowledge is vital to success.

But when a commodity trader goes looking for fundamental information to estimate the supply of and demand for a commodity in coming months, he finds himself in a maze. The amount of fundamental information on most commodities is almost boundless. It is also largely subjective and, therefore, open to a variety of interpretations. Even if a trader manages to sift through the fundamental information and arrive at a reasonable conclusion that prices are going to move significantly higher or lower in the next several weeks, he is still faced with two important decisions: (1) when to take his position in the market and (2) where to place a stop-loss order to bail him out if his fundamental analysis turns out to be wrong. Nothing in his fundamental considerations gives him any help here. Yet, because of the capital leverage inherent in minimum-margin commodity trading, these last two decisions can be just as crucial as his basic decision about which side of the market he wants to be on.

At this point the fundamental commodity trader is in psychologically the most uncomfortable decision-making situation possible—one in which there is no *a priori* knowledge available at all.

Techniques and Roulette

This situation and the typical human reaction to it are demonstrated in perfect microcosm by the gambling casino game of roulette. There are 37 numbers on a roulette wheel: 1 through 36 plus 0 (and 00 in the United States). With each spin of the wheel, the ball has an equal probability of landing in any one of the numbered slots. Unless the wheel is rigged (and he knows it), a player trying to decide where to place his bet has no clue whatsoever as to which number is likely to come up next.

Roulette players go to great lengths to escape the anxiety this situation creates. You often see players "charting" a roulette wheel by keeping a record of each number that comes up. Some casinos even provide printed cards to be used for this purpose, containing hundreds of tiny boxes to write the numbers in. The idea is that if a number—say, 28—hasn't come up in many spins of the wheel, the player bets that number because it is now "due."

To chart a roulette wheel in this fashion is tantamount to saying that the little white ball has a memory. Otherwise, the odds of 28 coming up on any one spin of the wheel are the same every time: 1 out of 37. It doesn't make any difference if 28 hasn't hit in the last 100,000 spins or the last million spins.

Anyone smart enough to have the money to finance a roulette game should also be smart enough to know he's kidding himself by charting the wheel. But he continues to do so for the same reason that other roulette players close their eyes and throw a chip on the table, playing it wherever it lands; or bet the same number—their birth date, their age, today's date, a "lucky" number—all evening long; or play for repeats, putting their chip(s) on the number that just came up; or make geometric patterns on the table with their chips, without regard for the numbers under the chips.

Why do roulette players behave in this strange fashion? To escape the responsibility for making the decision in an informational vacuum. By their actions they are telling us that when it's anybody's guess, even a meaningless method is better than none.

Filling a Need

Technical analysis of commodity prices, unlike the charting of a roulette wheel, is on a sound statistical footing. But it fulfills many of the same psychological needs. Technical analysis gives a commodity trader tangible reasons for choosing one price level over another at which to enter or leave a market, predicated on such historically valid considerations as price trends and price support and resistance levels. The pure technician, in fact, bases his trading decisions entirely on market action, theorizing that no matter what happens, it has to show up in the price chart, and when it does, he will interpret it there.

Most experienced traders probably have a foot in each camp, basing their broad trading decisions largely on fundamental analysis and using technical analysis to help in the timing of their trades. Regardless of what other purposes technical analysis serves or how its use is rationalized by a trader, wittingly or unwittingly it also serves a valuable psychological function by giving a trader an objective methodology for choosing from among the entire universe of price levels available to him a specific one at which he will buy or sell.

Herbert Lobel is a student of the market. At any time he can be found studying new techniques, reading obscure market literature, or devising his own methods for filtering or improving upon his favorite selected systems. He is a wealth of information. Mr. Lobel has been a commodity trader for many years. He is a graduate of Columbia University and of the famous Wyckoff Stock Market Course in advanced technical analysis, the Futures Trading course of the Association of Commodity Firms, in addition to attending programs at the New York Institute of Finance. Most of all, Mr. Lobel is a clear thinker and an expert game player. He excels in both chess and the handicapping of thoroughbred race horses. By combining the sucess of business, the analysis of education, and the candor of common sense, Herbert Lobel has much to teach the speculator.

"I can only say that I myself cannot trade intelligently without this form, which takes but a few minutes a night to complete. It tells you at one glance where you were, where you are, and where you hope to be." This statement, written in a letter accompanying Mr. Lobel's Worksheet, is still the best introduction to the idea. In the following pages Herbert Lobel presents a checklist method of organization which is important to all speculators. It is more generalized and complete than most forms you could devise yourself, and it has been refined over years of use. By recording all the details of the market and the systems that go into the daily decision-making process, the speculator disciplines him- or herself to a careful review; he or she has an actual record of the rationale that preceded trades and may evaluate the causes of sucesses and mistakes at a later time.

Mr. Lobel offers the reader more than just a record-keeping form. In his years of studying and trading he has reviewed many systems and extracted the features of some which are appealing to him; in other cases he combines approaches in order to validate the signals of individual methods. At varying stages of trading experience, each speculator attempts to weigh different systems and ideas that seem valuable. The author has taken a simple and effective approach to this problem and offers it as an intrinsic part of the Worksheet. *In doing this, the* Worksheet *becomes a system in itself.*

The Worksheet *is not intended to be a mathematical formula. The author's experience has taught him that not all decisions are quantifiable, even with the combination of well-defined systems. He offers the speculator a way of recording all the ideas and influences that enter into the trading decision. Some will choose to expand the columns, allowing comments relative to outside influences, but others may quantify everything.*

In arriving at his technique for combining methods, Mr. Lobel shares his experiences of studying many systems. He suggests the consideration of the ones he has found most interesting and valuable. He also explains his own method of testing the results and filtering these methods together in the section entitled Evaluation Performance, A Success-Failure Study. *If you have never attempted a consolidated daily worksheet, this is a good place to start; if you have one of your own, this may help you improve its use.*

THE DAILY DECISION-MAKER WORKSHEET

HERBERT LOBEL

The speculator, confronted in the arena of commodity trading by commercial hedgers and floor traders of all sizes and skills, in addition to competition from other speculators, requires effective tools for success in the decision-making process. It is not an easy task, since each trade in a diversified portfolio can be at a different stage: planning initial entry, pyramiding, or setting exit points. Because speculators use varying techniques and methods for the determination of stops and/or objectives, whether to preserve profits or to cut losses, an organized approach is essential.

Complicating the situation is the fact that the speculator's task does not stop at preplanning prior to the opening of each trading session. In addition to the "homework" he or she must do in preparation for the day, an effective means must be found to record the price action during the actual trading session. Following price movement is often necessary regardless of the degree of instructions given to a broker for the carrying out of the plans of the day (contingent entry points, stops, etc.). Most speculators like to know "what's going on?"

It is apparent that for intelligent decision making, and for effective observation of the ongoing marketplace, more is required than just miscellaneous scraps of paper on which the speculator jots various data. This article will present a simple organized form, a *Daily Decision-Maker Worksheet*, set up for each day of trading, on which the speculator can record by commodity:

1. The contract month (or months) which are being traded.

2. Any current open positions.

3. Technical data for the determination of entries and exits, stops, and the like. Further details on the nature of this technical data are discussed later.

4. A *Rating Method* for the technical data mentioned above, on the basis of which decisions can be made. Specifics about this *Rating Method* are also found later.

5. Any fundamental input, as distinct from technical.

6. Opinions or recommendations of any commodity services studied.

7. Analysis and final decisions as to new entries planned.

8. Final decisions as to which stops are to be used.

9. Any *new* positions entered that day, or *old* positions exited.

10. *Intra-day* quotes (highs, lows, and last) used for expanding intra-day entries or exits.

11. *Final* high, low, and close for the day, for use in plotting bar charts, point-and-figure charts, moving average or momentum; volume and open interest figures can also be entered, if required.

As will be noted, when all the above data is entered on the *Daily Decision-Maker Worksheet*—and that takes just a few minutes each day—the speculator can see at a glance "where he was yesterday, where he is today, and where he plans (or hopes!) to be tomorrow." At the end of each trading session he can observe the price action of today in relation to that of yesterday in order to check whether prices are up or down; he can compare the highs and lows of today with his recorded stops in order to check any new positions entered or old positions exited. All of this can, of course, be verified with his broker, who can confirm exact prices of entries or exits. Moreover, using the data on the *Worksheet* for each completed day, the trader can rapidly prepare the *Worksheet* for the next day, and plan his campaign based on the ever-changing facts before him.

The Worksheet

How and where to enter all the necessary data on the *Worksheet* and how to use it for planning is described later using the *Worksheets* illustrated in Figures 1 and 2. Some of the numerical entries are simple and routine; however, in Figure 2, column 8 *position signals*, column 9 *rating*, and column 7 *miscellaneous data* require definition at this point. Note that the spaces and columns on the *Worksheet* are not numbered from left to right, but are numbered serially according to the *chronological* sequence of entering the data in preparing the Worksheet each day. This preparation is described fully beginning in the section, *Recording the Advice of Services on the Worksheet* (p. 205).

The column headed *today's position signals* (Figure 1) contains, in symbol and numerical form, the positions (whether long, short, or neutral) and stops for those positions generated by whatever *technical* tools the speculator uses. Those tools may include moving averages, oscillators, momentum measures, swing analysis, and point-and-figure. In the *rating* column we set the numerical rating of the data recorded in the *position signals* column. The *miscellaneous data* column may contain, along with other data, any of the speculator's conclusions relative to bar chart indications for the particular commodity. For reasons that will be evident later, bar chart indications are set in a different column than point-and-figure, even though bar charts and point-and-figure charts are somewhat related, in the sense that they are each different means of recording price action.

Use of Technical Methods

Some speculators, depending on the time available and their personal inclinations, prepare and maintain their own bar charts, point-and-figure charts, moving average, oscillators, and other technical indicators. Others purchase charts from various commercial services, updating the charts themselves until the next issue. Many buy the output of computer services furnishing moving averages, point-and-figure charts, and oscil-

DAILY DECISION-MAKER WORKSHEET FOR _____ DAY _____ DATE

Today's Quotes	CO/New Pos. Today	Pres. Pos.	Prior CP	Today's Position Signals Contract Month	Commodity	Range	Rating	Misc. Data	Stop	Analysis- New Action
O H L LT				_____	WHEAT					
O H L LT				_____	CORN					
O H L LT				_____	BEANS					
O H L LT				_____	MEAL					
O H L LT				_____	OIL					
O H L LT				_____	CATTLE					
O H L				_____	BELLIES					

HOGS

SUGAR

COCOA

COPPER

NY SILVER

IMM GOLD

COTTON

LUMBER

O H L LT   O H L LT   O H L LT   O H L LT   O H L LT   O H L LT   O H L LT   O H L LT

FIGURE 1
Daily decision-maker worksheet form.

lators, together with trading recommendations based on those tools. Whatever approach or tools the individual speculator employs, it is essential that he or she test, by paper-trading over a two- or three-year span, the efficacy of any trading method based on those tools. The criteria to apply for testing of each commodity are:

1. Total net dollar profit after commissions (and return on margin).

2. Reliability (the percentage of successful trades to total trades).

3. Average profit per profitable trade (the dollar total of profitable trades divided by the number of profitable trades).

4. Average loss per loss trade (the dollar total of losing trades divided by the number of losing trades).

5. Maximum slump (the total of the maximum string of consecutive losses).

The lower the reliability of any given method, the larger must be the ratio of average profit per profitable trade to average loss per losing trade in order for the system to make money; a low reliability of only 30%, requires a ratio of 2.33:1 just to break even. With an attainable reliability of 50%, the ratio of average profit to average loss need be only 1:1 for breakeven. A realistic goal in the direction of cutting losses is a ratio greater than 1:1, with resultant net profits for the system.

Remember, of course, that *hypothetical* gains are one thing, and *actual* profits another. In actual trading, there are the inevitable bad executions and lock-limit moves that complicate entries and exits. You must allow for these problems in addition to allowing for commissions in your testing. As for the length of time over which the testing should span, it can only be said that the longer the better. Some technicians recommend as many as 400 trades for validity (5% error).

How to set up rules and to test those rules in a "success-failure" study are presented in the later section. First, we sketch through the various tools of technical analysis and, in a minor way, of fundamental analysis. Some source material, far from comprehensive, is also included, part of which may be new to some speculators. The discussion of technical and fundamental analysis which follows is not meant to be in any way complete; nevertheless, a review is necessary, so that one can have an overview of the parameters which enter into the decision-making process in commodity trading.

General Systems Overview

1978 saw the publication of three outstanding texts on technical analysis, each with a different point of view. P. J. Kaufman's *Commodity Trading Systems and Methods*, written at both elementary and advanced levels, is a pioneering work encompassing almost every field of technical analysis. John H. Hill's *Stock and Commodity Trend Trading by Advanced Technical Analysis* concentrates on the interpretation of daily bar chart action, including pivot point analysis and the Elliot wave theory. J. Welles Wilder's *New Concepts in Technical Trading Systems* is essentially the delineation of eight original commodity trading methods, the principles behind which are quite thought provoking.

Teweles, Harlow and Stone's *The Commodity Futures Game: Who Wins? Who Loses? Why?* and Stanley Kroll and Irwin Shisko's *The Commodity Futures Market Guide* are basic volumes dealing with virtually every aspect of commodity trading, both technical and fundamental. *Making Money in Commodities*, by Eugene Epstein, takes a critical view of the validity of widely accepted concepts. Houston Cox's *Concepts on Profits in Commodity Futures Trading*, with heavy emphasis on technical analysis, has much merit.

Bar Charting

Technical Analysis of Stock Prices, by Robert Edwards and John McGee, although dealing with stock prices, should be read at least once by every commodity speculator. The principles of supply and demand and volume indications are the same in stocks and commodities. *Forecasting Commodity Prices with Vertical Line Charts*, a monograph by William Jiler, is a simpler treatment of the same field. A little-known work by Kenneth Zinke, *New Technical Analysis of Commodities* (privately published) deals with some very original longer-term techniques in both bar charting and point-and-figure. David L. Markstein's *How to Chart Your Way to Stock Market Profits* is worthwhile reading, especially his volume-price trend analysis.

Commodity Price Charts (219 Parkade, Cedar Falls, Iowa, 50613), a separate weekly publication of *Commodities* magazine, offers a combination of daily bar charts, optimized point-and-figure charts, moving averages, cash and basis charts, and opinion commentary; weekly and monthly longer-term charts are also furnished. A fairly similar publication is from Commodity Research Bureau entitled *Commodity Chart Service* (Commodity Research Bureau, One Liberty Plaza, New York, New York, 10006). *Commodity Perspective* (327 South LaSalle Street, Chicago, Illinois, 60604), concentrating on only daily bar charts and commentary, has excellent small-scale grids for the meticulous charter.

Point-and-Figure

The Chartcraft Method of Point-and-Figure Trading, by A. W. Cohen, utilizes varying box sizes for different commodities. In 1970, Professors Robert E. Davis and Charles C. Thiel, Jr. of Purdue published an historic book, *Point-and-Figure Commodity Trading: A Computer Evaluation*. It challenged the standard three-box reversal standard and detailed the results of optimizing box units and reversal numbers for 15 commodities. The improvement in profits was startling. In 1975 K. C. Zieg and P. J. Kaufman, in their volume *Point-and-Figure Commodity Trading Techniques*, did further trail-blazing work in optimizing point-and-figure parameters and presented valuable techniques for both beginner and advanced point-and-figure traders. *Chart for Profit*, by Earl Blumenthal, adds some interesting facts to the field of point-and-figure trading.

Moving Averages and Oscillators

The books mentioned under the *General Systems Overview* section of technical analysis deal with the construction and use of moving averages and oscillators. Victoria Feed Co. of Davenport, Iowa has published material on their 4-9-18 day moving average crossover method. A recent important contributor to the field of moving averages is Frank Hochheimer, author of the 1978 *CRB Yearbook* article, "Computers Can Help You Trade The Commodity Market," elaborating on the results of his moving average research. That work has been supplemented by his "Channels and Crossovers" (Commodity Research Report published by Merrill Lynch Pierce Fenner and Smith, Inc., July 1978) in which he details further results on the same subject.* In February

---

* The two primary works by Mr. Hochheimer can be found in this volume in their entirety.

1979 Mr. Hochheimer released a third study, "Computerized Trading Techniques," summarizing and expanding his previous works.

No discussion of moving average source material would be complete without mention of Richard Donchian, whose *5- and 20-day moving average system* has a long historic record. Two West Coast researchers who have developed unique variations of moving averages are James Sibbet, with his *Cumulative Average,* and John Herrick, with his *VECMAM (Variable Error Correction Moving Average, Modulated).* Sibbet is also prime developer of the application of contrary opinion to commodity trading * and cofounder of a composite-type of bar charting service (Market Vane, 61 S. Lake Avenue, Pasadena, CA 91101, and Sibbet-Hadady Publications, same address).

One of the finest technicians in stock market technical analysis is Gerald Appel. Among his best works are *New Directions in Technical Analysis* and *Winning Market Systems,* both of which deal in part with moving averages and oscillators. The first book mentioned contains an excellent explanation of how to construct exponentially smoothed moving averages.

The *Commodity Research Bureau Daily Trend Analyzer* (Commodity Research Bureau, One Liberty Plaza, New York, New York, 10006) publishes buy and sell signals based on the use of several moving averages of price action. Commodex (114 Liberty Street, New York, New York, 10006) has a similar service that also incorporates data based on volume and open interest considerations, in addition to that based on price action.

Swing chart analysis, really an offshoot of bar charting, with its dependence on the penetration of support and resistance points for buy and sell signals, was popularized by some of the now classic technicians (W. D. Gann, William Dunnigan, H. M. Gartley, etc.), and can be found in their writings.

Cycles, Seasonals, Odds and Historic Price Ranges

It is certainly great to have a buy or sell signal indicated by some combination of moving averages or oscillator systems, point-and-figure,

* See "Using Contrary Opinion in the Commodity Market," by R. Earl Hadady, pp. 115–132 in this book.

swing charting, or bar chart analysis. To further contribute to the success of that particular signal in producing profits, it would be ideal if the commodity was at a cyclic low at the time of the buy signal, e.g., the seasonal trend should be up, and the odds (the probability of an up-move, based on a study of similar calendar periods in the past) should be in favor of the position. In addition, it would be helpful if the current price of the commodity is in the lowest quadrant, or perhaps the lower half of its historic price range, measured from 1974 onward (after the giant inflationary leap upward in general commodity prices in 1972–1973).

It must, nevertheless, be carefully interjected here that it is rare to find a long or short position signal supported by every conceivable technical factor. It is more realistic that, at the time of a given signal, some factors may favor the position while others may not. This is precisely where the *Daily Decision-Maker Worksheet* plays its role by bringing together all relevant data on one organized sheet, so that the speculator can form an intelligent judgment, all pro and con factors being considered, as to the probable success of the contemplated trade.

Returning to the subjects of cycles, seasonals, odds, and historic price ranges—four contemporary commodity analysts have done outstanding specialty work in these areas. Walt Bressert, of HAL Commodity Cycles (P.O. Box 2275, Evergreen, Colorado 80439), is a leading expert in advanced commodity cyclic and seasonal analysis. He is closely followed in the area by Jake Bernstein of M.B.H. Commodity Advisors (M.B.H. Publications, P.O. Box 383, Winnetka, Illinois, 60093). Both men have also published commendable and useful cyclic and seasonal studies. Bruce Gould, author of the *Dow Jones Irwin Guide to Commodities Trading* and the *Commodity Trading Manual* (privately printed), plus an essentially educational periodical publication, *Bruce Gould on Commodities* (P.O. Box 16, Seattle, Washington, 98111), has done extensive work on seasonals and odds, including the evaluation of basis.

Other Technical Approaches

There are many advanced techniques which the sophisticated speculator can use in his arsenal of methods. Those techniques include, among others, Elliot wave analysis, Fibonacci-Lucas numbers, spectral analysis, and the esoteric studies of David Harahus. W. D. Gann has published a wealth of meaningful material. It all depends on how "involved" the individual wishes to get!

P. J. Kaufman's previously mentioned *Commodity Trading Systems and Methods* incorporates most of the advanced thinking in the field.

Fundamental Input to the Worksheet

The crucial fundamental interplay of supply and demand does move the markets. However, it is often very difficult for the speculator first determine accurately the fundamentals at any particular time, and then to interpret correctly those fundamentals. On the other hand, the net effect of the fundamentalist supply-demand equation must, now or ultimately, be reflected in the price, volume and open interest charts, for evaluation by the technical analyst. Some technicians, of course, like to add some fundamental input to their decision making. The *Daily Decision-Maker Worksheet* has, therefore, space in the *miscellaneous data* column for inclusion of that input. Dates of any impending crop reports and certainly fundamental input should be set at the right time in that *miscellaneous data column* (this is especially useful for those traders who do not wish to hold a position through a major report, for whatever reason).

For those speculators who prefer a service that provides fundamental information to point the way to a possibly winning trade—to which timing of entry and exit can be applied by technical tools—Gerald Gold, author of one of the first general texts in commodity trading, *Modern Commodity Futures Trading*, publishes a highly interesting periodical entitled *Selected Commodity Trades* (P.O. Box 1279, Old Village Station, Great Neck, New York, 11023).

Recording the Advice of Services on the Worksheet

The review of technical and fundamental sources of information contained in these last sections involves a prolonged study by the speculator. The recommendations and opinions of those services will vary from day to day or week to week, depending on the frequency of information output and the nature of the analysis. It will be helpful to summarize such services' opinions of any given commodity with brief symbols that can then be set in the *miscellaneous data* column of the *Daily Decision-Maker Worksheet*. The following are some suggestions:

+ *Bullish*
++ *Very bullish*
− *Bearish*
−− *Very bearish*
+? *Bullish IF certain conditions met*
−? *Bearish IF certain conditions met*
? *Indecisive*
S.T. *Short term implications*
L.T. *Long term implications*

We are all familiar with the occasional "hedged" comments in services (i.e., trying to cover the situation whether the commodity goes up *or* down), hence the necessity for some of the qualified symbols.

Any other useful data that can be gleaned from services, in the opinion of the speculator, such as current market position, long (L) or short (SH); its entry recommendations, buy (B) or sell short (SS); recommended exits to sell (S) or cover short (CS); or recommended stops (STP), can also be set in the *miscellaneous data* column. That does not mean that the speculator will necessarily follow all that advice. The input will simply be considered in his final decision for entries, exits and stops, depending on the combination of the tools used for making the decision. The stop-loss to use for each position, when finally determined, is set in the *stop* column, and decisions relative to entries, exits, and the like set in the *analysis-new action* column. All this is illustrated later, when the *Worksheet* is prepared step-by-step.

We can now continue with the further detailing of the *position signals* column which, as will be recalled, contains in symbolic and numeric form the positions (whether long, short, or neutral) and stops for those positions generated by whatever *technical* tools the speculator uses. In proceeding, it is first important to understand "filtering," the strategic philosophy that permits the combining of more than one type of technical input resulting in a single trading decision.

Filtering Methods Together

If a trader depends on only one technical system (moving averages, oscillator, point-and-figure, or bar chart indications), the resulting performance relates to the efficacy of that one system alone. To reach a decision, many sophisticated traders add a second technical method, and often a third, for several reasons. For entry indications, the additional methods can sometimes eliminate possibly losing trades, by not entering those positions if the signals of those additional "editing" methods are contrary (or even neutral) to the signal of the first method. Should the second and third methods agree with the entry signal of the first method, we have further validation, although not a guarantee of success.

When exit decisions use the signals of more than one method, the combination of signals can give added confirmation. Using more than one method can also help cut "shrinkage," where large unrealized profits can turn into far smaller realized profits. For example, if the trader is using system A, based on slow moving averages and has accumulated substantial profits in a position, the employment of method B, based on moving averages of higher speed, could result in an exit from the trade prior to giving back much of those profits. That same early exit may also have been accomplished by the use of point-and-figure signals instead of a faster moving average. But filtering more than one method may result in confusion and indecision unless specific rules are established for acting or not acting on the combination of signals. In addition, the individual methods must be tested, at least in theoretical trading (actual trading is preferred) to verify that they yield profits. This section will show how to set up and test those rules.

Examples Combining Three Methods

For the purposes of illustrating the use of three systems in combination, we will define method A as a medium-speed moving average method, generating relatively slow signals. Method B is a technique using both moving averages and oscillators but with signals considerably faster than method A. Method C is based on an optimized point-and-figure chart, entirely different than A or B. We also assume that methods A and B are "band-methods," which will allow them to have a neutral or sideways state as well as giving buy and sell signals.   Point-and-figure, of course, must be either long or short, never neutral.

The three methods above are only selected to help make the points clearer.   The speculator can set the signals for whatever technical methods he or she chooses in the *position signal* column, using the symbols which follow, and the *rating* details to be described after that.   To place signals in a limited space, such as the *position signal* column, requires the use of symbols, to which are added appropriate numbers (for stops, prices, etc.).   For methods A and B we use the following symbols, and select one of these values for calculating the *ratings:*

   ↑ Up or long, value of 2 points
   = Neutral or sideways, value of 1 point
   ↓ Down or short, value of 0 points

For method C, point-and-figure, we use a different set of symbols, to differentiate it from methods A and B:

   + Up or long
   — Down or short

You will note that the point-and-figure symbols are not assigned any numerical value, but the + or − is simply added to the *rating* when the latter is calculated.   As an example of how the *rating* is set up—a very simple procedure—suppose we have:

Method	*A*	*B*	*C*
Direction	↑	↑	+

Add 2 points for A and 2 points for B, which equals 4; then add the + for method C (point-and-figure), and the resultant *rating* is 4+, which is entered in the *rating* column on the *Worksheet.*

It is very helpful to keep the point-and-figure rating (+ or −) separate and not added to the values of methods A and B (i.e. not a rating of $2 + 2 + 2 = 6$ as in the above example).   Point-and-figure can be regarded as either the exceeding of resistance of the breaking of support, whereas methods A and B, in the example, are based on different parameters.   We will see that method C, point-and-figure, can be decisive in situations where the signals of methods A and B are not yet conclusive.

The following are additional examples of how to figure the *rating:*

(Note we always keep the signals of A, B, and C in the same order, from left to right)

Method	A	B	C	Rating
(1)	↓	↓	—	0—
(2)	↑	=	+	3+
(3)	=	=	+	2+

Expanding the Notation

Prices can be entered near each symbol to give important information, as follows:

Method	A	B	C	Rating
	↑ 232½	↑ 228	+220½	4+
	208	216¼	207	

For long positions, the stops dictated by each of the methods are set *under* each symbol (as 208, 216¼, and 207 for methods A, B, and C, respectively). The 232½, 228, and 220½ to the *right* of each symbol are the prices at which each method entered their individual long positions. It should be stressed that any one of those stops, and any one of those entry points, is not necessarily the stop used by the speculator on that day for his own position, nor is it necessarily the price at which he entered his own position. The stops entered for each method, along with other information on the *Worksheet*, simply help him reach a decision, and that decision is entered in the *stop* column. The entry point for each of the methods is useful to record because, for reasons to be discussed later, the trader may sometimes delay his entry into a position, and he will often look back to see where each method entered.

Consider another example, showing the use of numbers placed around the symbols:

Method	A	B	C	Rating
	512	510	518	
	↓ 508	=	— 522	1—
		499	490 ReSS	

Method A went short at 508, with a present stop of 512. Method B is sideways (neutral), and will be long at 510 or short at 499, depending on the day's action. Method C is short from 522, with a stop at 518. The "*ReSS*" means that there will be a *repeat* short sale signal at 490. As point-and-figure traders know, a repeat signal is often possible in either short or long point-and-figure positions, and can be used for pyramiding if validated by other data. (If point-and-figure is +, any *repeat* long signal is written *above* the +, e.g. 562 *ReB*.)

One final example shows the use of symbols and numbers to illustrate a new trend change. Suppose that prior to a Monday's market action the symbols were

Method	*A*	*B*	*C*	*Rating*
	341	345		
	↓	338	+335	1+
		=	329½	

Monday is a strong up day, and the stops of methods A and B are hit, resulting in trend changes. The symbols and rating for Tuesday's guidance on the *Worksheet* would appear as follows:

Method	*A*	*B*	*C*	*Rating*
	346	↑ 345	+335	3+
	= 342	new	329½	
	new	328		
	334½			

The *new* on the right of the methods A and B symbols, together with the 342 price of entry for method A, indicates the new trend change. Method A is now sideways and will be long at 346 or short at 334½ (if neither price is touched during Tuesday's price action, method A signal will still be sideways for Wednesday's action). Method B has turned up at 345, with stop at 328; point-and-figure remains up with a stop at 329½.

Two points about the symbols and numbers: the daily work can be abbreviated by not recording the entry point numbers at the right of each symbol every day. That step is necessary only if the trader thinks that information is important for the decisions of that day. The examples also imply that, for methods A and B, the action signals and stops are intra-day. That is not always true. In some methods, action signals and stops are on a close-only basis, acted upon only when the closing price satisfies the criteria. Method C, point-and-figure, is always on an intra-day basis, by the nature of its rules.

Interpreting the Ratings

It is evident, from the illustrations of symbols and numbers, that on any given day the several methods employed by the trader can vary from each other in their signals. Certainly it would be very pat if all three methods were continually in the same direction or poised for trend change on a given day, but the reality is unfortunately otherwise. Interestingly enough, in a recent situation in December 1978 corn, that fairly rare coincidence did take place. After the market action of Wednesday, September 27, 1978, with a close on Wednesday of 223½, the signals for December corn set on the *Decision-Maker Worksheet* for Thursday, September 28, were:

Method	A	B	C	Rating
	225½	225	226	2—
	=	= new	—	
	218½	219¾		

The high, low, and close for Thursday, September 28, were 226½, 223½, 226. The result was a 4+ buy signal, which could be acted upon that day. For Friday, September 29, the symbols appeared as:

Method	A	B	C	Rating
	↑ 225½	↑ 225	+226	4+
	new	new	new	
	217¾	221¾	217	

The coincidence of signals on the same day is not very frequent, but this realistic example helps to make clearer position signal entries in a sequence of days. Because the ratings can vary anywhere from 0— to 4+ with 18 different possible combinations of symbols, it is now important to detail those 18 combinations and the *rating* of each. We then discuss the all-important matter of how to use the symbols and ratings as entry or exit signals in trading and how to test the rules you formulate. (See Table 1.)

TABLE 1 RATINGS AND ACTION FOR COMBINED SIGNALS

	A	B	C	Rating	[1] Entry	[2] Exit
BUY	↑	↑	+	4+	B or HL	
	↑	↑	−	4−	B	S (see text)[5]
	=	↑	+	3+	B	S (see text)[5]
	↑	=	+	3+	B	S (see text)[5]
NO ACTION ZONE	=	↑	−	3−	W [3]	
	↑	=	−	3−	W [3]	
	=	=	+	2+	W	
	=	=	−	2−	W	
	↑	↓	+	2+	W	
	↓	↑	+	2+	W	
	↑	↓	−	2−	W	
	↓	↑	−	2−	W	
	=	↓	+	1+	W [4]	
	↓	=	+	1+	W [4]	
SELL SHORT	=	↓	−	1−	SS	CS (see text)[6]
	↓	=	−	1−	SS	CS (see text)[6]
	↓	↓	+	0+	SS	CS (see text)[6]
	↓	↓	−	0−	SS or HS	

Abbrev: B Buy Long   SS Sell Short   S Sell Long   CS Cover Short
HL Hold Long   HS Hold Short   W Wait (no action)

[1] For a long position, on moving up from a lower rating to a higher rating; for short position, on moving down from a higher rating to a lower rating.   [2] For long position, on moving down from a higher rating to a lower rating; for short position, on moving up from a lower rating to a higher rating.   [3] At *bottoms*, 3− might be satisfactory for a Buy signal.   [4] At tops, 1+ might be satisfactory for a sell short signal.   [5] RATING could in one trading session deteriorate to as low as 2− (= = −) but that is rare.   [6] RATING could in one trading session improve to as high as 2+ (= = +) but that is rare.

Let us consider first *buy* signals. No action is taken in the *No Action Zone*. When the *rating* improves to 3+, 4− or 4+ we buy. Note that 4− ratings are rare in a situation of increasing ratings, for usually by the time methods A and B have both turned up, method C, point-and-figure, has turned up. *Ratings* of 4− are mostly sell signals, often after a good bull move, when method C, point-and-figure, turns down first.

The question will immediately be asked—does one buy on a 3+ rating (i.e., before both methods A and B have turned up), or is it best to wait for the highest bullish rating of 4+? The answer depends on the outcome of the trader's tests using his own methods.

Success-Failure Studies

Under certain circumstances, when following a long-established bear move, the maximum ultimate profit may be in taking a long position when the *ratings* have improved to a 3— (= ↑ — or ↑ = —.) Here methods A and B have improved from what was certainly a 0— at the bottom of the move (↓ ↓ —), but point-and-figure has not yet turned. The decision to buy on the 3— rating would depend on verification by other factors, such as bar chart indications, cyclic or seasonal data. In any event, buying on a 3— should be tested against back data, as should any new rules in a system, using success-failure study.

Note the symbols under each of the methods A, B, and C in Table 1. Two of those methods are, as stated on previous pages, based on moving averages and/or oscillators (A and B), and one is based on point-and-figure (C). The 18 possible combinations of symbols are valued, and the *ratings* calculated, according to the system set forth in the section *Filtering Methods Together* and *Examples Combining Three Methods*. The *ratings* are then ranked in Table 1 with the 4+ most *bullish rating* at the top, down to the 0— most *bearish rating* at the bottom.

Entry and Exit Signals

When categorizing signals, *entry signals* (buy or sell short) are considered separately from *exit signals* (sell or cover short). Note in Table 1 the *No Action Zone*, which includes the middle 10 combinations, from the rating 3— to 1+. Those 10 *ratings* require no action to be taken of either buying or selling. The ratings are neither bullish nor bearish enough, or the individual symbols are in opposite directions. It should be stated here that, in success-failure research done with the ratings as to their effectiveness as buy or sell signals, the highest frequency of failures, and the highest total loss, came from the four 2+ and 2— ratings of (↑ ↓ +) (↓ ↑ +) (↑ ↓ —) and (↑ ↓ —) the most indecisive of all the *ratings*. One must wait for a change in the *rating*, of the proper type and magnitude in either direction, before acting.

In considering the liquidation of long positions we see that the *exit* column in Table 1 indicates a sell S for either the 4— or 3+ ratings, when there has been a deterioration from the 4+ rating. But a long position is liquidated for one of two reasons:

1. To cut further losses of a losing position.
2. To preserve profits in a winning position.

It is not relevant that the trader's motivation in (2) may be that he expects a decline, or has reached a predetermined objective.

In situation (1), when cutting a loss, some judgment can be used by the speculator as to whether to sell if the rating drops (e.g., from 4+ to 4— or 3+). If he has figured his risk-reward ratio for the trade and the maximum risk (loss) he wishes to take has not been reached, he might decide to stay with the long position, at least until his maximum risk is reached. By holding the position, the price action might improve, and the rating increase to a 4+ again; but, under any circumstances, the deterioration of a rating should be regarded as a warning to look more closely at the position. Staying with the position after a decrease in rating might prevent some whipsawing at times, especially when using a "fast" moving average which may soon change direction again with a higher rating and a new or reentry signal. Yet to completely ignore a lower rating and liquidation signal can lead to large losses.

Different criteria are applied to situation (2), where the trade has a profit, and the trader wishes to liquidate to preserve profits. Although one could consider whether or not one's profit objective for the trade has been reached at the time the rating dropped, and the sell signal occurred, it is best to always sell to preserve profits. A profit is a profit. If prices turn up again, and the rating improves to a buy signal, one can always reenter. On the other hand, the price action might continue against the speculator and profits could be lost. The sequence of symbols and ratings might go as follows, after the original buy signal:

From	↑	↑ +	(4 + buy)
to	↑	= +	(3 + sell)
to	↑	↓ +	(2+)

Note, however, that we do not go short on the 2+ rating   We are in the *No Action Zone,* and our rules keep us out of the market until we again enter either the *Buy* or *Sell* zones.

Using the symbols and ratings for going short (see the bottom of Table 1) and covering those shorts, is exactly the reverse of going long, then selling those longs. We sell short in the *Sell Short Zone,* and cover on an improvement in *rating.* All the other discussions about long positions apply in reverse to selling short. It will be good exercise for the reader to now review the previous discussion of long positions and apply the "mirror image" to selling short and covering.

The principles of buying and selling short, as detailed in this discussion, are predicated on buying on price advances, and selling short on price declines. That serves as verification of strength or weakness, the basis of trend trading—going with the trend. Admittedly, there are other methods that seek to buy on weakness and sell short on strength. In commodity trading more than one type of method, or a combination, can be successful. What should be tried is a union of the two diametrically opposed philosophies: buying or not buying on the proper rating signal, as per Table 1; but, under any circumstances, positions are taken or compounded on some predetermined amount of reaction, *provided the rating has not deteriorated.* The same applies in reverse to short positions, of course.

Dennis Dunn and Edwin Hargitt, in their excellent *Trader's Notebook,* have included a discussion of several interesting techniques for buying on reactions and selling on short rallies, including those of George Cole and William Dunnigan. Zieg and Kaufman, in their *Point-and-Figure Commodity Trading Techniques,* present some facts about how to use point-and-figure in a similar way.

Evaluating Performance, a Success-Failure Study

Reference has been made earlier to testing by employing a success-failure study. To illustrate a success-failure study, let us take an actual example. We discussed the possible options of buying long on a 3+ or a 4— rating before a 4+ rating is reached (or, similarly, selling short on a 1— or a 0+ *rating* before a 0— *rating* is reached). Suppose a set of rules for a given commodity using a success-failure study:

Rule 1, Entry Rule: Buy long only *on a 4+ rating. Do not buy on 4— or 3+ ratings. Wait for the 4+ to be reached.*

Rule 2, Exit Rule: Sell out a long position immediately on any diminution of rating (as a 4—, 3+, etc.).

Use a data bank of back signals for as long a period as possible. If you have a limited history of signals for the three methods you are testing, then simulate as if you were trading in the actual market, using your current signals. For maximum validity, combine the two types of testing.

Multicolumn pads (up to 22 columns), on white background, horizontally ruled, are available in most commercial office supply stores. Assign your "slowest-moving method," called method A, to the left-hand quarter of the pad; assign method B, the "faster-moving method," to the next quarter portion to the right; assign the next quarter to method C, point-and-figure, or whatever "method C" you are using in your technical work. Leave the right-hand quarter for your analysis and any notes.

We first tabulate method A, in order of entry date and exit date with corresponding entry and exit prices. When a long signal existed, place a ↑ symbol next to that trade. If method A was neutral (sideways), do not enter any data for that period; blank horizontal lines will mean that the method had no position for that period. (You can, if you wish, put the = symbol denoting "sideways" on those blank lines). If the next trade in method A is a short sale, tabulate the entry date and price and exit date and price for the period during which the short signal existed; place a ↓ symbol for that trade.

Follow the same procedure for methods B and C (using the + and − symbols if the method is point-and-figure). Then set up your analysis columns on the right as follows, using rules 1 and 2 for entry and exit:

Success Trades		*Failure Trades*	
Made profit (by waiting for 4+)	Avoided loss (by not buying on 4− or 3+)	Suffered loss (by waiting for 4+)	Missed additional profit (by not buying earlier on a 4− or 3+

Enter the dollar amounts for each successful trade and each losing trade. Analyze the "pure" net result, first without considering other factors; then go back and analyze, for each trade, any bar-chart indications, cyclical or seasonal factors, or probabilities that existed. Enter those factors in the *analysis* column next to the appropriate trade. Your conclusion might have been, from the "pure" results you obtained from the success-failure study for a given commodity, that it is best to wait for

a 4+ rating before buying; but closer analysis of trades when 3+ or 4−
ratings existed for entry signals (remember that a 4− entry signal is
rare, and you will be studying mostly 3+ signals here for entry) may
reveal that it is more profitable, overall, to buy early on the 3+ or 4−
signals in the event of an accumulation bottom, combined with some
favorable cyclical, seasonal, or probabilities factors.

In evaluating any method, record for any given period:

1. The total net profit and return on margin
2. The percentage of successful trades to total trades (reliability)
3. The average profitable trade and average losing trade
4. The maximum slump

A similar success-failure study, only in reverse, should be done to test
whether early entry into a trade, when a 1− or 0+ rating exists is more
feasible than waiting for a 0− rating to take a short position.

In commodity trading, just as in the scientific handicapping of thoroughbred race horses, a *composite* approach should be used in the decision-
making process. *Composite* means that as many factors as possible
should be taken into account, both those that can be quantified and those
that cannot be reduced to precise numbers. In handicapping those factors include current condition, speed, class, pace, weight, post position,
jockey, trainer, running styles of the contestants, distance, track condition, and racing angles. In commodity trading the factors are more
numerous, and the technical analyst must apply similar inductive
and deductive reasoning, within his sphere, in estimating the probabilities of profit potential for any contemplated trade (exactly as
a skilled handicapper estimates the probabilities of any one horse
being the winner). Therefore, in any trade *try to have as many positive
factors going for you as possible.* That is the principle behind the
4+/0− thinking—and the *Daily Decision-Maker Worksheet* can, if
properly used, help you toward that end. It points toward the good
trades, and eliminates the less favorable ones.

Preparing the Daily Worksheet

Let us now turn to the actual preparation of the *Daily Decision-Maker
Worksheet*. Figure 1 reproduced the blank worksheet, with no details
entered for the reader's convenience in making up his or her own *Worksheet*. Figure 2 shows the *Worksheet* with some examples filled in, and

DAILY DECISION-MAKER WORKSHEET FOR ① DAY ② DATE

Today's Quotes ⑫	CO/New Pos. Today ⑬	Pres. Pos. ⑥	Prior CP ④ ⑤	Contract Month ③ ⑭	Commodity	Range ⑧	Rating ⑨	Misc. Data ⑦	Stop ⑩	Analysis-New Action ⑪
O H L LT					WHEAT					
O H L LT	CS 223	5H 225	220¾	DEC	CORN 218	225 223 226 ═ ↓225 -223 224 221¼ 223¼	1—	BC- BOTTOM X — Y 5H STP 225 Z—	CS 223	INTERDAY
O H L LT					BEANS					
O H L LT			54.60	DEC	CATTLE	5560 5630 5590 ═ 5530 5380 -5590 55.10 54.70 54.92	2—	BC- BEARISH Crop Report— X= Y— Z—		FAVOR SHORT. SALE DEPENDS ON SIGNALS

218

FIGURE 2
Daily decision-maker worksheet with example data.

Feb BELLIES

O	H	L	LT
2	63.40		68.02

ODDS 85% ↑ X+L 63.30 X+H B 6750 REACTION
4 ↑
Feb ___ BELLIES ___ OL OL ReB 73.10 ↑ 64.00 67.25 67.75
STOP OL
5 MIT 69.50 OBJECTIVE REACHED
68.50

SUGAR

O	H	L	LT
			65.00

Dec COPPER

O	H	L	LT

2 ↑
Dec ___ COPPER ___ 63.30 ↓ 66.10 ↑ 63.80 64.00 64.20
64.80
WAIT FOR DEFINITIVE DIRECTION

Dec COTTON

O	H	L	LT
B#(2) 65.30	L 64.70		64.77

SEASONAL ↑ BARCHART + X + Y++L 6460 Z +
3 ↑
Dec ___ COTTON ___ 65.28 ↑64.60 +64.20 = 62.42 63.10 63.70 65.40
STP (#1) 63.70
BUY ADD (#2) DEC CLOSE OVER 65.28
65.64 64.95

LUMBER

O	H	L	LT

219

the spaces or boxes numbered in the order in which the *Worksheet* is prepared each day.

The examples given are hypothetical and are solely intended to give some idea of the various ratings which can result from the symbols. Not all commodities are filled in.

Preparation is in the following order:

1. Enter the day of week.

2. Enter the date. Tuesday's *Worksheet*, for example, will be prepared after Monday's close, and will contain the signals and ratings resulting from Monday's market action. The information on the *Worksheet* for Tuesday will be used in the decision-making for Tuesday's action.

3. Enter *Contract Month* in which you are trading. If trading is in more than one month simultaneously, within the same commodity, or by spreading, the second month can be entered under the first month, and all data for that month written in on that lower line. Commodities can be added or deleted, of course, depending on actual trading.

4. Enter the previous trading day's date. CP stands for the closing price.

5. Enter the previous day's closing price. Those traders who use the previous day's high, low, and close for guides in trading today may prefer to enter the previous day's high and low in this space, in addition to the close. However, such entries might clutter up the *Worksheet* too much. The trader can always refer back, if necessary, to the previous day's *Worksheet* which, as is noted later, has the high, low, and close for that day prominently written in *red*.

6. Enter any current open positions and price. Use L for long and SH for short.

7. *Misc. Data:* Enter any relevant data concerning recommendations or positions—L long, S short, B buy, SS short sale, STP stop, and so on. Services are referred to in the example as X, Y, or Z. Enter any data on seasonals, cycles, probabilities, bar chart indications, and any fundamental input, including crop report dates, and the like. This is a "catchall" column, depending on the tools each trader utilizes.

8. Enter your *Position Signals* here. Position signals have been fully covered in the text.

9. Enter the calculated rating.

10. Enter here the *Stop(s)* you have finally decided to use for your present open positions—S sell long, CS cover short. *Those stops may or may not coincide with the stops of your position signals or services.* Your final stop is selected, based on your judgment, after study of all input. Any stops to be used for entering new positions can be set in the *Analysis-New Action* column.

11. *Analysis-New Action:* We are now ready, by referring to most of the pertinent data entered in the columns to the left, to finalize plans for any anticipated *new* positions to be entered. Those plans are recorded in this *Analysis-New Action* column, together with any other conclusions you have reached in reviewing the Worksheet. We are now ready for today!

12. *Today's Quotes:* Today's market action has started. Record here details you receive from your broker as to the opening range 0, and any interim quotes of the H high, L low and LT last. Older quotes can be crossed out, and more recent ones written in. If you follow the quotes at various critical times, those important quotes can be underlined or otherwise marked.

13. Enter here prices at which you closed out. CO any old positions today, and prices at which you took any new positions today—bought B, sold short SS, sold out long S, or covered short CS on information from your broker.

14. The trading day is over. Here you enter in *red*, so that it stands out, the final high, low, and close for the day. From both the interim quotes on the *Worksheet* and this final high, low, and close you can detremine at a glance whether any of your interpreted stops or the stops of methods A, B, or C were hit at any stage of the trading. The high, low, and close data can also be used for your bar charting and point-and-figure.

A review of the *Daily Decision-Maker Worksheet* will reveal that it truly tries to do the job of telling you *where you were, where you are, and where you plan to be,* as stated earlier in the text.

Bernard Baruch once introduced himself to an investigating committee as a "speculator and investor." Asked to define the speculator, he described him as the man who takes a view of the future and acts on it. We agree that to *speculate* is to commit oneself after having formulated a hypothesis on presumably rational grounds, whereas to *gamble* consists merely of tossing a coin or acting on a hunch after having made a conjecture at best. Your *Daily Decision-Maker Worksheet* can be a very valuable commodity trading tool in helping you to formulate a hypothesis on presumably rational grounds so that you can attain maximum net profits. Try it!

INDEX